Stand Up
for Your People
SECOND EDITION

GABRIEL SHARP

Stand Up for Your People
SECOND EDITION

Copyright © 2020 Gabriel Sharp

All rights reserved. No part of this book may be reproduced in any written, electronic, recording, or photocopying form without written permission from the publisher. Please do not participate in or encourage piracy of copyrighted materials in violation of the author's rights. Purchase only authorized editions.

ISBN: 978-0-9997662-8-6

10 9 8 7 6 5 4 3 2 1

Printed in the United States of America

Library of Congress Control Number: 2019919484

Author: Gabriel Sharp

Edited by: Fiesta Publishing

Cover Design and Interior Layout: Alli Masi

Cover Painting: Gabriel Sharp

Cover Photograph: Jim Sullivan, J. Sullivan Productions

Fiesta Publishing
fiestapublishing.com

DEDICATION

Dedicated to Walks in Faith.
You showed me the way.
May you walk in harmony forever on the Red Road.

OPENING PRAYER
by Walks in Faith

Grandfather,

I am growing tired from worry and doubt. My mother and father are ill and have seen many moons. I miss my brothers and sister; but most of all, my children. I am far from my home, the reservation. It's been many long years.

Have pity on me Grandfather, make me strong again. Renew my faith in your promise to keep my loved ones safe, so long as I love and worship only you.

Grandfather, bless my brothers in the same manner. They are all here with me and I am almost certain we suffer the same struggles.

Grandfather, bless our sisters who live in these big houses as well.

Grandfather, do not hide your beauty from us as we seek you in all things. Bless us to live in harmony and be at peace with each other, to respect all things as sacred and to love one another.

Grandfather, hear my prayer, for I am pitiful and lowly.

Mitakuye Oyas'in

TABLE OF CONTENTS

Prologue	9
The Native American Sweat Lodge	17
Native American History	61
The American Prison System	97
Ceremonies, Sacred Items and Religious Freedoms	141
Court Cases	181
Solutions	217
Native American Rights Survey	239
Final Word	245
Acknowledgements	247
About the Author	249
References	251

PROLOGUE

INTRODUCTION
by Grey Bear

I am half Native American. My mother was white and my father was full-blooded Mohave Indian. As part of the Mohave Tribe my family lived in Parker, Arizona, along the Colorado River. We are known as the *Pipa Aha Makav,* the River People. I lived on the reservation with my parents and siblings until I was five years old when we moved to Tempe, Arizona, a suburb of Phoenix.

Once off the reservation, I was taught a history that was not of my people. I remember my third-grade teacher announced to the class that we were going to skip the chapter in the history books that concerned Native Americans. She said it wasn't necessary and looking back, the textbooks we used in school glossed over the complete history of Native American oppression. So, I learned about Native American history on my own.

I learned about the American Indian wars by reading books that my parents had in our house when I was a teenager. During my ten years of incarceration I read books about the American Indian Movement and the struggle for Native American civil rights. I learned that my father participated in the AIM (American Indian Movement) Occupation of Alcatraz.

Growing up, I was a poor student because I didn't study or take school seriously. I stayed away from the Native way because I was not fully exposed to it while I was living in a primarily Caucasian dominated environment. I struggled to find myself through other means by reading about my people while living in a society not my own. I never thought to look in the mirror to see who I was and am.

Whenever there was a funeral, my father Gabriel, my brother and I would return to Parker. My father was a Medicine Man and I remember how he sang Mohave songs, called Bird Song, as he played a gourd before, during and after the funeral. He would sing Bird Song all weekend, as singing assists the spirit of those who have passed away to move onto the spirit world.

When we reached the reservation on the way to the ceremony, he removed his abalone shell from his medicine bundle and we prayed by the side of the road. He was a very spiritual person. He used an eagle feather to fan smoldering sage (smudge). He prayed to the Great Spirit and Mother Earth. He prayed for the Four Directions and for our people. My father taught us kindness, respect and patience.

My mother Paulette worked for the Inter Tribal Council of Arizona (ITCA). When I visited her at work, her office desk was messy; piles of policies and legal papers everywhere. She had a Master's Degree in social work and worked as a policy director for the Inter Tribal Council of Arizona (ITCA). ITCA established itself as a voice for tribal governments in Arizona.

While incarcerated I practiced my Native American religion and experienced the desecration of the sacred sweat lodge area by prison officials. They also removed the water drum permanently, repeatedly desecrated the sacred objects, made it difficult to obtain firewood for sweat ceremonies, and required proof of race before my Native brothers or I were allowed to practice our religion. These violations prompted me to respond in the best way I knew how, by writing.

I filed grievances on behalf of Native American rights. I wrote letters to anyone who would show interest or empathy for the Native American religious right cause. I created prison zines (pamphlets) called the *Native American Prisoners Journal,* which were then sent to Chicago for printing and nationwide distribution. Eventually, I filed a lawsuit in Federal Court over religious freedom issues for Native American prisoners. The lawsuit resulted in settlements and a judgement granted in favor for the Native American prisoners. The zines and court papers became the foundation for this book, *Stand Up for Your People*.

I decided that the Native American religious rights story must be told. During the process of telling the story, a lot of research had to be done, as there was very little information available about incarcerated Native American prisoners. I began to focus on available information about Native American oppression, which started with our history.

There are few writings about Native American religious rights in prison. I sourced information from law books, family and friends, and searched online for any reference to Native American prisoners. I created a survey asking Native American prisoners questions related to their religious rights, so advocates outside of prison would know what's really going on. I created the survey with the hope that someday someone will have the desire to use it, or a similar survey, to start the information sharing process. The survey is also a tool for Native American prisoners to use when asking for help when writing to people on the outside.

There were many Native American prisoners who assisted me in writing this book, both by providing advice and inspiration and by sharing their writings which are in the book. I attended many sweat ceremonies and talking circles with these fellows. I lived in the same dorm as three of them. All of them went home after finishing their sentence.

Walks in Faith

Walks in Faith was my cousin and person to show me the *Red Road* (spiritual path toward redemption). He became the pipe holder at the one of the prisons where I was incarcerated. He introduced me on how to sing Native American traditional song. He was family and I loved him as such. He traveled to the spirit world shortly after I was released from prison and he left his Native American friends a pathway to the Red Road for us all to follow. Walks in Faith contributed the opening prayer for the book and was with me in meetings with the prison Chaplain and with the Warden of the prison.

Spotted Owl

Spotted Owl and I shared a bunk briefly at one of the prisons and he became one of my best friends. He spent a lot of time learning about his own tribal background and Native American religion. Spotted Owl shared his research on Native American history for this book, which helped me get started on my own research. He was released from prison and now makes Native American crafts for his livelihood.

Grey Deer

Grey Deer was an elder member of the Havasupai tribe who lived in the same prison cell area as me. He used to advocate for Native American religious rights, however he stopped filing complaints after being placed in solitary confinement. John was beaten up by white inmates because he was willing to speak up. Grey Deer contributed some hard to find Arizona Department of Corrections prison policies that were valuable in the court case mentioned in this book and encouraged me to stand up for our rights.

Eagle

Eagle was the first pipe holder at the prison where I completed my sentence. He was the caretaker of the sweat lodge and filed the grievance paperwork when it was desecrated; which lead to him being sent to another prison shortly thereafter. His removal resulted in Walks in Faith being voted as the next pipe holder.

Disclaimer: With over five-hundred and seventy federally recognized tribes and nearly seventy State recognized Native American Tribes in the United States, the history shared in this book is related to a handful of Tribes located in and around Arizona giving context to the historical struggles of Native Americans who live in Arizona. There are many traumatic events that have shadowed all the Native American Tribes in the United States and the history presented is not intended to slight any Tribe and the struggles they endured at the hand of European discoverers and settlers.

HOME ON THE REZ
by Grey Bear

The hum of the van's engine seems to get louder as the radio starts to die out. Once you get out of Phoenix, you have an hour before the radio stops picking up the transmissions. I was very quiet. Usually I just stared out the window watching the clouds and the desert.

In the desert I could see all the animals dancing around, cavorting to things unknown to human senses. In the clouds, dragons and giant eagles soared and splashed. My father was as quiet as me, I wondered if he could see the same things from my imagination. He turned right, northward off the main highway to a smaller road. The signs read that we were headed toward either to LA or Las Vegas, but we wouldn't reach either. The scenery changed a bit. Out here, there were no cities, only mountains and desert. This was heaven for the animals, birds and creepy crawlers that lived in this desert, one of the last refuges away from human encroachment.

After a little while, during the drive to the reservation my dad would tell me to get his gourd. It was in the back of the van somewhere. I searched inside a pouch that rattled when it moved and I knew it was either a rattlesnake or his gourd. I took it to the front of the van and opened the pouch turning my head away from it, afraid of what I might find. It was one of my father's gourds. This one was blue, as large around as a grapefruit with a stake of wood for the handle.

I already knew what to do. I started to shake it in a tap-switch motion at a certain pace. Tap-swish, tap-swish. Hon-dah, hon-dah, hon-dah, high-way, hon-dah, hon-dah, hon-dah, high-way.

It was dad's hot dog highway song that he would sing to me and my brother, as it was the only song that we knew how to sing. I would ask him to sing was about an eagle too. The eagle would fly up into the sky and would look for and find another eagle, so the two eagles could fly together. He would also sing songs three nights in a row at a Mohave's funeral, while I would hang around outside playing with cousins around the *Cry House* (funeral home).

On the drive to Parker, he would practice singing many songs in his baritone voice. The gourd was giant in my young hands. While he sang he would signal again, which meant for me to roll the gourd steadily in a circle for a few seconds for a chorus where he picked up the pitch of his voice, then went back to normal. After a few verses he made a harrumph sound to signal the song was coming to the end. "Harrumph-hmm-hmm", at the end of the song as I shook the gourd hard with three final strokes. "That's to wake up the people who fell asleep during the song," he would always tell me.

My father knew an endless stream of songs. He would sing as we cruised down the highway and passed a sign that read, *Welcome to the Colorado River Indian Reservation.* It was a large white sign with the tribal seal on it. I remember the sign because one time when we were young, my brother and I were sitting under the sign when we were attacked by an army of ants. As I sat on top of an ant hill, my dad picked me up and made me take off my pants while he brushed off the black ants. When my brother and I were older, he recalled that he was the only person who sat on top of the ant pile; but I remember differently – picking those critters out of my Masters of the Universe underwear.

Sometime after entering the Colorado River Indian Reservation, dad would pull off the road at a certain location. He would retrieve a large leather bag, his medicine bag, from one of the back seats of the van. It had a certain smell to it, a combination of sweet grass, sage and cedar. He had a large shiny abalone shell in which he would place some sage, then light it. He prayed to the Great Spirit and gave an offering of smoke upward with an eagle feather, he prayed for the spirits of the Four Directions and gave offerings of smoke to each, and then he crouched and gave an offering to Mother Earth. He gave a prayer to our people and he gave a prayer for his family. We survive as children of Mother Earth.

He prayed for the two and four-legged creepy crawlers, two winged and those that swim; all depend on her for survival. The deserts, forests, mountains and rivers nourish us. Father Sky shines down upon us with the sun, brings rain to keep the planet alive. When we make a smoke offering to the different elements of the desert, we are releasing those leaves to another state of composition. We establish a connection between Mother Earth, Father Sky, the Great Spirit and the Universe. We burn and rub the smoke on our bodies; we breathe the smoke and become part of the connection. My father told me it was like making a phone call to the Great Spirit and we were the phone.

He gave the ashes back to Mother Earth; put everything back in his medicine bag, which I returned to the back of his big white van. I got in and closed the door. We drove into Parker with the radio off.

THE NATIVE AMERICAN SWEAT LODGE

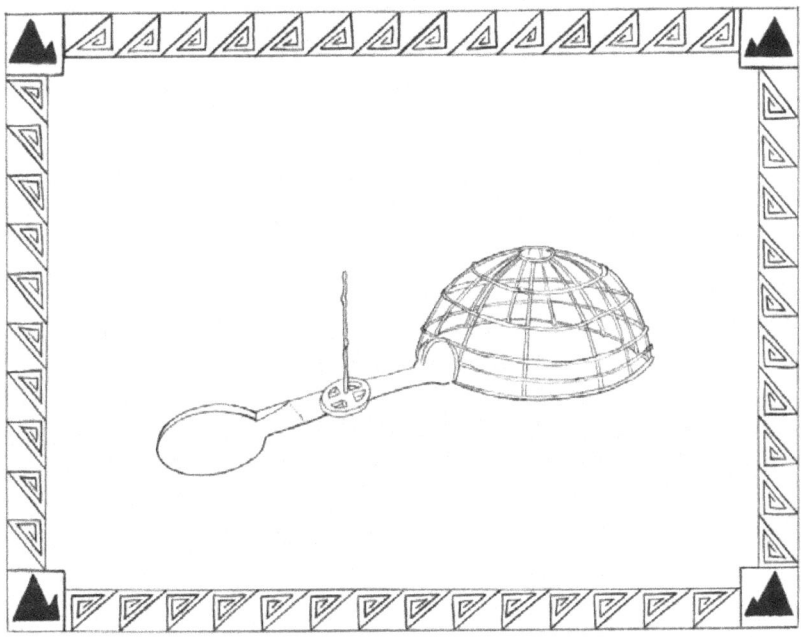

THE SWEAT LODGE CEREMONY: MY PERSONAL EXPERIENCE
by Grey Bear

I didn't know much about the sweat ceremony, but when I was in Junior High, I read a lot about the various tribes in the United States and my father would practice Native American religion by smudging. It wasn't until I was incarcerated at thirty years old that I saw a sweat lodge. I didn't know what it was, or its purpose, so prison was where I learned about the sweat lodge, it's purpose and how to conduct a ceremony.

I had only been incarcerated for a week when a Native brother asked if I was going to sweat with them on the weekend. He then said, "Come out to the lodge this weekend, bro" and "If you need anything like soap or shampoo, let us know." So, as a newly incarcerated Native American, I attended the sweat lodge ceremony the first Saturday I was in prison.

The sweat lodge is a place for purification and rebirth for Native Americans. Historically, it is a widespread tradition that ranged from the Aztecs in Mexico to the Inuit in North America. The sweat lodge was created to purify the body, cure illnesses, to influence spirits, and to pray for the ones who need the prayers. We sweat, so we can purify our bodies and suffer for our prayers. During the sweat ceremony, the Creator (God) breathes his hot breath upon the participants. The pain that one experiences with the sweat is a release of the fear, anxiety and sadness that the person is undergoing in their life. The members suffer for their loved ones, so they won't.

The sweat lodge ceremony is the core ceremony that Native American spiritual practitioners use in order to gather for traditional religious purposes. As a ritual purification ceremony, it helps with mental, emotional and physical restructuring. The sweat ceremony is also an opportunity for Native Americans to orally pass down traditions by teaching, learning Native American values and beliefs, and sharing history with others without using a writing or recording device. The spoken word is memorized and the receiver of information then passes it to the next person, orally as well.

Ever since my first sweat experience, I have regularly sweated with my Native American brothers in prison. All the Native Americans stood in a circle and took turns introducing themselves to me. I was treated like family, more like a long lost relative. No one in the circle held any rank over another. We were all equals combined in blood and spirit. They didn't judge me negatively because I was unfamiliar with the *Native Way*. After two sweats, I began to assist with the preparation and caretaking of the fire that is used to heat the lava rocks at the sweat ceremony. I did this on a weekly basis and continued helping for the next two years where I was incarcerated.

In 2010, I, Grey Bear was moved to a new unit in a private prison. As I began to spend more time attending ceremonies and sweating in the new lodge, I tried to initiate more opportunities for the brothers to gather in ceremony but was denied by officials without receiving an explanation for the denial.

I believed the denials were grossly unfair in the prison because the Christians had many *turnouts* (time slots to practice religion) during the week to attend their ceremonies, while the Native Americas were restricted to no more than one religious activity a week.

At the time, the Arizona Department of Corrections (ADOC) policy had provisions for extra functions for religious groups, but this only happened for the Christian groups. Chaplains and other officials in prison often openly discriminated against non-Christian religious groups (Jewish and Muslim, etc.)

The sweat ceremony in an ADOC prison is allowed once a week, although it rarely happened more than once a month. Native Americans who asked for special sweats for holidays or special occasions were generally denied by prison officials. Finally, since the policy leaves sweat lodge frequency vague, some prisons rarely get to use their sweat lodge at all.

The frequency of the sweat lodge ceremony depends on three things:

- The availability of resources such as wood, lava rocks, water, tools for working with the hot rocks, and willow poles for the sweat lodge.

- Communication with staff for access to the sweat lodge area and for access to the tools necessary to conduct the ceremony.

- Proper policy to guarantee the first two requirements. If the Native brothers have a sweat ceremony every week then they are blessed.

The lack of a firewood policy became a major issue while I was incarcerated. Prison officials used various tactics to prevent Native Americans from getting wood. For many weeks a sweat didn't take place because officers denied the brothers the use of a hammer. The hammer was needed so the recycled pallets could be broken down in order to make firewood for the ceremony. Ultimately, the wood supply was permanently cut off and the officers who helped us previously with the wood were ordered to stop.

The Arizona Native Americans could go months without a sweat ceremony in prison. This is because the process for people to donate wood is onerous. Talking to Native Americans that came from other prisons, they also informed me of the difficulties of obtaining firewood for the sweats.

Prison officials would not allow the replacement of lava rocks forcing the Native Americans to use (burn) the rocks until they became too small to be effective. Sacred herbs were available on a very limited basis and herbs necessary for a sweat were denied. It can take up to three months for ADOC officials in property and the religious department to approve and allow the herbs. Prison protocol allowed for only one ounce of each herb at a time.

The long processing time is due to having only one religious department for each ADOC prison and only one Christian chaplain who is placed in charge of all religious services at each prison. Inevitably, this leads to favoritism for the Christian religious groups; which can have multiple branches or denominations at any prison.

The prison land on which the sweat lodge is located is sacred ground. To the Native American, the prison officials cannot own that land, because no one can own the heart of Mother Earth. Instead, the land is to be respected and this includes prison searches, as they are policy and part of institutional life. But, a search of the sweat lodge led to its desecration because it was not conducted in a manner that was respectful of Native American religious belief. Searches of Native American religious boxes, which are associated with the sweat lodge ceremony, were also desecrated on many occasions. It got to the point where some Native American prisoners wouldn't keep religious objects because they would become desecrated.

Often, the rules were easily bent and ignored. I found the ADOC policy, or lack thereof, to be unjust and biased. I realized that ADOC religious policy must be set in writing to protect all religious practice in a fair manner. With the Red Road before me, I used my knowledge as a paralegal and brought a lawsuit against the Arizona Department of Corrections.

CHAPTER 1

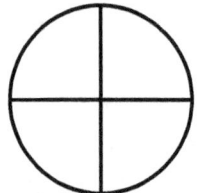

THE SWEAT LODGE RITUAL

Building a Sweat Lodge in Prison

When building and blessing a sweat lodge in prison, if possible, a Native American Spiritual Advisor is the best person to consult. If an advisor is not available within the prison system, there may be Native American inmates who have adequate experience to build and bless a sweat lodge at the discretion of the group.

The sweat lodge should be located in a quiet area that has low foot-traffic. The area should be at least fifty-feet by fifty-feet, with a fence around it to protect the sacred area from desecration. Once the physical area of a sweat lodge is established, it is considered sacred land by the Native Americans. When a Native person walks onto the religious area, it is as if he/she is stepping back into their homeland.

The land, willow poles, lava rocks, firewood and accompanying utensils used to perform a sweat ceremony are all considered sacred and when building the lodge, Native American protocol needs to be followed.

The components required to build a sweat lodge in prison are:

> • Tarps and blankets – The number depends on the size of the sweat lodge and the size of the blankets. Generally, fifteen to twenty large blankets.

- Twenty willow poles – The poles should be replaced annually.
- Lava rocks – The rocks should be replaced every six to twelve months.
- Four – 12" rock forks – Used to move hot rocks.
- Firewood – Need to have a regular supply based on sweat frequency.
- Shovel, pitchfork, hose, two large water buckets and a dipper (buffalo horn or gourd).

The frame of the sweat lodge is built in a dome shape using the willow poles. The frame is configured so a doorway will open to the east. Most sweat lodges are designed this way because the sun rises from the east and represents the power of the Creator. Several layers of blankets are then placed over the framework and a door is made over the frame doorway. A person outside the sweat lodge is designated to help open and close the *flap* (door) for those sweating inside.

Sweat Ceremony in Prison

The Arizona Department of Corrections allows sweat ceremonies for its inmates, but some states do not allow sweat lodges for incarcerated Native Americans. A group of inmates who were part of the Massachusetts Native American Spiritual Awareness Council filed a claim stating that they were subject to discrimination by prison administrators. In the 1995 court case, Trapp, et al. v. Dubois, et al. was able to obtain a sweat lodge through the court system. This is one example of several court cases where Native American prisoners had to sue the prison for their religious rights.

From start to finish it takes about four hours to set up, conduct the ceremony, have a prison count and return the equipment. Once a ceremony has been started it cannot be interrupted. However, the conductor does plan for the Native Americans to a take break in between each sweat lodge round and for prison head counts.

Every Saturday morning, the Native Americans are released from their prison cell early so they can eat breakfast, then head to the sweat lodge ground. The fire starters are the first people to arrive so they can prepare the fire pit in advance of the other inmates arriving. The fire starter's responsibility is to gather the wood, jugs, buckets and blankets. To make the fire pit, they count the number of lava rocks that the conductor has requested for the sweat ceremony. The wood is sorted and the fire starters begin to build a fire by adding wood to make it the size needed, adding rocks as they build. After the fire pit is ready, blankets are placed over the entire *inipi* (Lakota word for sweat lodge). When the inipi is ready, the fire starters wait for their brothers to arrive from the *chow hall* (cafeteria) and prepare for the sweat.

The Sweat Lodge Ritual

There are different ways to learn about the sweat lodge ritual including oral tradition, participation or by reading books. For inmates, the prison will usually have a process to allow books to be delivered from the outside. Grey Bear recommends *The Sacred Pipe,* recorded and edited by Joseph Epes Brown, which can be ordered from a variety of stores. There are several stores where Native American books can be mail ordered. Oral history or talking to other Native Americans about the sweat ceremony is also a great way to learn because tribal history can be shared.

But the best way to learn about a sweat lodge ceremony, is to participate in one. Everyone who participates in a sweat lodge ceremony needs to remember that it's not an endurance test to see who is the bravest, strongest, or how long one can stay inside the inipi. Every Native American brother's sweat lodge ceremony is different, so in prison, the brothers teach and learn from each other. Since there are different ways to conduct the ceremony due to the many different tribes represented in prison, an intertribal ceremony is conducted. When a Medicine Man enters a prison from the outside, he sweats and passes his teachings onto the brothers when he conducts the ceremony. When he speaks, all participants listen to what he is saying as it helps others to conduct the ceremony when he isn't present.

"I've conducted sweat lodge ceremonies and have been the conductor's helper. Every time I sweat, conduct, or am a helper, I learn something new. After my release, I taught my Native American friends how the sweat lodge ceremony is conducted in prison and passed on what I learned, so they can pass it on to their children," Grey Bear states.

Sweat Ceremony Preparation

Each conductor runs their sweat lodge ritual according to the way they have been taught, so each sweat is conducted differently. While the inmates change into the clothes they will wear during the ceremony, they prepare themselves by socializing and practicing Native American gourd and drum songs. The conductor gathers his shell that holds sage, cedar or sweet grass, and blesses the ceremonial grounds. The conductor's helper goes to the fire pit with his pinch of *kinnikinnick* (special tobacco), stands to the east and offers a prayer and places the *pinch* on the fire pit wood. The helper then places a pinch of the kinnikinnick on the wood in the fire pit in a clockwise direction for each of the Four Directions. East, South, West and North. From the east, he then offers a pinch to the Creator and places it in the center of the wood pile.

While the helper blesses the fire pit, wood and rocks, the conductor blesses the grounds, inipi and altar. The conductor then places the shell he was using on the altar and joins his helper on the east side of the wood by the fire pit. The conductor lights the fire from the east and they move clockwise around the wood, lighting the fire. Then they bless the sweat lodge. The entire process takes about thirty minutes before the rocks are ready and the brothers can enter the sweat lodge.

The conductor will roll more kinnikinnick in a cornhusk, light it, then enter the inipi through the left side of the entrance way. He crawls on his hands and knees clockwise until he is sitting by the entrance way. The fire pit is a three-foot diameter circle located in the center of the sweat lodge where the hot lava rocks are placed. All movement in a sweat ceremony happens clockwise in honor of the Sun and the Cycle of Life. Clockwise is also known as *sunwise* to Native Americans.

The helper enters from the left side and sits down to the left of the entrance way while the conductor sits to the right of it. Both are facing inward toward the fire where the rocks will be placed. Above them, in the center of the sweat lodge is the Sacred Hoop. This is a circle of willow poles on the roof and is said to be a pathway to the universe, a conduit to the spirit world, or a connection to the Creator.

A fire starter pulls the blankets over the opening, thus closing the entrance way of the inipi. This makeshift doorway is also called *the flap* and makes the sweat lodge dark inside. The conductor lights a *rolled smoke* (cigarette) made from kinnikinnick and offers the smoke as a blessing to the Creator, Mother Earth and the Four Directions. He says a prayer out loud and smudges himself at the same time by fanning the smoke onto himself. When he is done saying his prayer, he passes the kinnikinnick to his helper, who then says his own prayer. The two remain in the inipi until the Kinnikinnick is almost gone and they have both recited their prayers.

The two call out for the fire starter to lift the blankets. The conductor exits the sweat lodge from the right side, takes the remaining Kinnikinnick smoked, and walks sunwise around the fire pit where the fire is burning, and gives the rest of the Kinnikinnick to the fire as an offering.

The conductor's helper crawls sunwise in the inipi and exits out the right side. The conductor takes a cup of water from the bucket of water used during the ceremony to make steam and makes a water line from inside the inipi, over to the altar and fire pit, which are located directly east from the sweat lodge door. The water line represents an umbilical cord from Mother Earth's womb, which is represented by the sweat lodge and is connected to the fire that heats the rocks.

Once the water line is made, everyone waits until the wood is ready for the sweat ceremony to start. While the brothers wait for the ceremony to start, they sing Pow Wow songs, Peyote song, and Bird Song using a large drum, a small drum, gourds and instruments. They take off their shirts, so they are only wearing their gym shorts when they enter the lodge. The ADOC has dress requirements which state that male inmates must wear orange gym shorts during a sweat ceremony.

The fire starter will tell the conductor when the rocks are ready, who in turn will tell all the Native brothers it's time to start the sweat ceremony. The conductor says a prayer to the Creator before he enters the inipi. Following sunwise protocol, the conductor is the first to enter. One by one all the other Native brothers enter the same way and sit on the north, west and south sides of the inipi, wherever there is a place to sit. Once everyone is seated, the helper is the last to enter the inipi and sits south of the doorway.

The fire starter then hands the herb-filled shell to the helper, who then passes it to the brother sitting on his left. The shell is passed brother to brother sunwise until it reaches the conductor. The fire starter then hands the *rock forks* to the helper inside the inipi. Rock forks are wood sticks that are about one inch in diameter that are split into prongs at the end. The fire starter or his helper, remove the rocks out of the hot coals using a shovel and metal rake, transferring the glowing red hot rocks onto another shovel. The ashes are blown or brushed off with a rag before they are taken to the inipi to prevent the ashes from blowing loose in the sweat lodge.

When the fire keeper's helper takes the shovel with seven rocks into the inipi, he stays south of the water line. When he gets to the entrance, he lets the conductor and his helper know he is there by saying loudly, "Aho! Rocks!" which means, "Here are the rocks!" As he brings the rocks into the inipi, he touches the shovel with the rocks to the pole that is in the center of the altar. The pole or staff in the center of the altar is called the *staff of life*. The conductor or his helper guide the shovel with the glowing rocks to the edge of the rock pit. The helper then uses the rock forks to remove the rocks from the shovel and places them into the rock pit.

The conductor takes the first rock and motions it in a clockwise round motion in the rock pit which is in front of him and sets it in the center. The first rock represents the Universe or Grandfather. The second rock represents all the children in the world and is placed to the east of the fire pit. The third rock is positioned to the south and it is for the women in the world. The fourth rock is placed to the west and represents medicine or healing. The fifth rock is positioned to the north and is for the warriors, those who have fallen in battles and for the ones who are fighting now.

Next, a rock is placed between the north and east rocks for Mother Earth and the last rock is placed between the east and south rocks for the Native inmates and their people (family and friends). Each time the conductor's helper places a rock in its respective spot, he makes a sunwise circle with it. Then the conductor teaches the attendees about a tradition that he has learned from others.

Once all the preparation is completed, the sweat lodge ceremony is ready to begin.

Rules to Sweat By

When Grey Bear arrived at the prison and met his Native American brothers for the first time, he was handed a piece of paper with the following rules for participating in a sweat lodge ceremony. He doesn't know who wrote the rules or when they were written, but anyone who participates in a sweat ceremony is handed the following guidelines.

- No card playing or game playing during any ceremony.
- No radios, TVs, or tape recorders played during any ceremony.
- No arguing or fighting around sacred grounds and during a ceremony.
- No drugs or alcohol around the sacred grounds or used during a ceremony.
- No one under the influence of drugs or alcohol in the sacred grounds or present in any ceremony.
- No physical or verbal abuse or disrespect shown to anyone present in the sacred grounds or around the sacred items at any time.
- No cussing around sacred grounds and items.

- No spitting, sitting, standing on, or throwing of sweat lodge rocks and wood.

- No cigarette butts or trash thrown in the sweat lodge fire pit at any time.

- Always offer tobacco (even if it's from a cigarette) to the outside people who attend a ceremony with you.

- No disrespect or discrimination shown to any brother or sister regardless of tribal affiliation or blood quantum.

- Feathers are not to touch the ground, except when placed on the altar in a respectful manner.

- Everyone attending the ceremony must help in the preparation, each person takes responsibility for getting water, wood, assisting the pipe holder, tending the fire, etc. in a quiet and cooperative manner. No one is to sit around.

- Keep the sweat lodge area clean and neat at all times.

- Keep all the sacred items in a clean area, protected from other people, and in a place where they will not be abused.

- No negative talk about women or disrespect shown towards them at any time, including other female inmates, female staff and female visitors.

- No women on their moon (menstrual period) allowed around the sacred items and grounds during their flow and for at least four days afterwards, including female staff.

- Do not use the ceremonial times as a way of getting out of your cell or dorm. Everyone present at a ceremony must participate.

- Show respect to all brothers and sisters on the yard twenty-four hours a day, every day.

During Grey Bear's years in prison, he saw all these rules broken by the Native inmates, including himself. What is important to realize when one messes up, admit that you can do better, then make the right decision the next time an opportunity presents itself.

CHAPTER 2

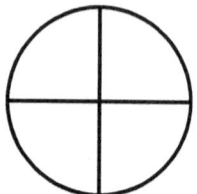

SWEAT LODGE CEREMONIES AND PRISON

The Sweat Ceremony Experience

When the conductor is ready to begin, he tells the fire keeper to bring the first set of rocks. The rocks for the ceremony are placed in the rock pit in no specific order. The conductor then places a pinch of cedar on each rock in the rock pit for a blessing.

The conductor passes the shell with herbs out the doorway to the fire keeper outside. Then the conductor's helper passes the rock forks around so that each brother can touch them before they are handed outside of the inipi and placed in a bucket of water until the next round. Next, the fire keeper hands the drum, the drumstick and gourd to the conductor's helper, who is inside the inipi.

A bucket of water is also handed inside, taking care to keep it elevated above the ground. The conductor and his helper take the water bucket between them, touch the rocks with it, then set it between them. The fire keeper closes the flap and the sweat lodge fills with the darkness of the Universe. The rocks glow red with ancient knowledge. The lodge is checked to ensure that no light enters the inipi. In complete darkness the conductor and helper are ready to begin the first of four ceremonial rounds.

The first round is the children's round and starts with the conductor thanking the brothers for joining in the ceremony.

The conductor prays for all the brother's children and the children of the Red Nation. He prays for all children of the world, and then he gives his helper the opportunity to pray for the children, as well. After the conductor's helper is finished with his prayers, he might sing a song, or he may pass the drum, drumstick and gourd to the brother to his left.

The conductor makes a water blessing by splashing water four times on the rocks, creating the breath of the Great Spirit (God). The breath is the steam created by the water landing on the hot rocks. For some it can be uncomfortable, while for others it can be soothing. How the steam feels to a participant depends on what they carry in their heart when they enter the inipi. This could include positive or negative thoughts that they may have about something or someone for whom they want to pray. They may feel strong emotions such as anxiety, sadness, or grief. The sweat lodge is a place to release these difficult emotions.

Depending on the guidelines set by the conductor, each brother may say a prayer out loud, sing, or pass the instruments. Everyone prays for what is important to them. The drum, drumstick and gourd are passed from each brother sunwise until the items reach the conductor. During each round usually four songs are sung as each person prays, while the conductor and his helper splash water blessings periodically to keep the heat going.

When the instruments are returned to the conductor, he says a prayer and may sing a song before he ends the children's round. Ending the round he says, "On the count of three; one, two, three," and everyone says in a loud voice, *"Mitakuye Oyas'in!"* (Lakota statement that means, *all my relations* and indicates that we are all related to each other in some manner), so the people outside the lodge can hear and know when to open the flap.

The flap is raised from the outside. The conductor and helper hand the bucket of water to the fire starter, then the conductor hands out the ceremonial tools, including the gourd and drum. The helper gets up and crawls sunwise around the rock pit in front of the brothers. One by one the brothers exit according to tradition until the all the participants have exited. The last one to leave the inipi is the conductor.

As everyone exits, they immerse their arms in a bucket of water to cool down. They walk sunwise around the fire pit to an area where they can cool off with water from a hose, drink water and rest on the ground. Care is taken not to cross the water line that runs between the fire pit and where the wood is kept burning to the rock pit inside the inipi, out of respect for Mother Earth. Ten to fifteen minutes is allotted between rounds, so the brothers can cool off and the rocks become hot for the next round. "Aho!" the conductor calls to indicate the second round. The conductor enters the inipi first from the left side and the other brothers follow.

The second round follows the same pattern as the first, except the conductor and his helper pray for the womenfolk. This includes mothers, sisters, wives, daughters, girlfriends and other womenfolk in the men's lives. The brothers pray for Mother Earth, for her healing and protection. The instruments get passed and they sing and pray for the womenfolk. *Aho Mitakuye Oyas'in!* Steam floats off the brother's bodies as they crawl out. Brothers help brothers with water and a towel for a spot to lay down and rest. The fire keeper puts more wood on the fire.

During the break between the second and third rounds the brothers wait for prison security to conduct a count. Coordination between the required prison count and the third round can be difficult. Within the prison system, the security officers on duty change all the time, so how an officer conducts a head count of the sweat lodge participants can also differ depending who is on duty.

Once the prison has completed its count and the lodge is prepared, the third round for medicine and healing begins. The Native inmates pray for the Creator to strengthen their healing implements, such as the herbs, the sacred pipe and the sweat lodge. They pray for healing of those in their families and for others. After the third round, they exit the inipi and rest until the rocks are ready. Sometimes the conductor may decide that there will not be a break between rounds.

The third round, which is the medicine round involves praying, smudging and smoking for strength and healing. Smudging involves burning herbs such as sage or cedar and using the smoke for healing or blessing. It's up to the conductor to decide where to conduct the medicine circle, outside or inside the inipi.

If the round is held outside, the participants stand in a circle. Since smoking is involved in this round, either a rolled smoke made from a cornhusk or rolling papers and kinnikinnick, or the sacred pipe is used. The conductor starts by lighting the pipe or rolled kinnikinnick with an ember from the fire, he puffs and offers the smoke to Grandfather (God), Mother Earth and the Four Directions.

He uses the smoke to smudge himself, then passes it to the brother to the left of him who smudges himself in the same way and the rolled smoke is passed around the circle. The conductor takes water from a bucket and offers it to Mother Earth by splashing it from his hand to her. He takes a sip from the jug of the *water of life* which represents all water. It is passed around the circle along with a medicinal tea made from sage and other herbs.

Drinking the herbal tea is like smudging, using sacred herbs to spiritually cleanse oneself. The conductor blesses the drum, gourd, water and the medicinal tea. At this time he will also bless objects for the brothers, such as a bandana, medicine bag, feather, gourd, drum or sometimes pictures.

The brothers often say a prayer when they are smudging and blessing themselves. After all the medicine items, the drum, gourd and sometimes a feather or feather fan have made their way around the circle, the conductor will take a shovel with embers from the fire, add some cedar and rolled smoke and walk sunwise blessing the altar, staff of life and sweat lodge by touching them with the shovel and smoke. Then, the brothers sweat.

If the medicine ceremony is conducted inside the sweat lodge, the brothers enter as protocol requires. The shell with herbs is passed to the conductor from outside the inipi, while the drum, gourd, drumstick, water and tea are given to the conductor's assistant. The conductor's helper uses one of the rock forks to draw in the dirt a medicine wheel inside the entrance way of the inipi. The conductor places a pinch of cedar in the middle of the medicine wheel.

Native American Medicine Wheel

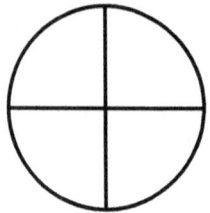

The Native American medicine wheel is a form used by many different tribes to represent the Four Directions and the Sacred Hoop. The directions have specific meanings that are significant to the person praying. The Native inmates chose to have the wheel represent children, women, warriors and *spiritual medicine* (healing).

The fire keeper brings a flat hot rock to the inipi where the helper transfers it with the rock forks to the medicine wheel, in between the conductor and the helper. The rock burns the cedar on the medicine wheel giving an offering to the Four Directions and the rock represents the Native American's ancestor. The conductor puts a pinch of cedar on the rock, which burns and blesses the sweat lodge with smoke; the helper blesses the instruments and drinks a blend of water and tea with the smoke.

The conductor then uses the rolled kinnikinnick or sacred pipe and blesses it with the cedar smoke, while he continues to add pinches of cedar to keep the smoke going. The helper motions the rolled or pipe smoke towards each of the Four Directions, then he puffs smoke onto the ceremonial items to bless them. He offers the smoke to the Creator, Mother Earth, Four Directions and for his own spirit, then passes the smoke to his brother to the left of him.

As the smoke works its way around the inipi, the helper offers and drinks some of water and medicinal tea and passes it to the left, in a sunwise manner. When the items reach the conductor, he offers his prayers and smudges himself in the same manner as everyone in the sweat lodge. Then he passes the items out the doorway to a brother standing outside of the inipi, where all the brothers who aren't sweating are standing in a line. When the last brother on the outside finishes his blessings, he gets a pinch of cedar, walks to the fire pit, and makes an offering by using smoke and cedar. The offerings are to the Creator, God and Mother Earth. It is not set in stone who an individual's offerings is offered to; it depends on the person making the offering. A lot of the ceremony is ritual practice, the specifics are left open for the individual practitioner to create for themselves.

The grounds can be blessed with smoke by carrying a shovel that has embers and cedar on it around the inipi and altar. The conductor may ask for the water line to be remade at this time. Afterwards, he uses the shovel to pick up the rock on the medicine wheel and place it on the east side of the fire pit. He says, "Aho!" when it is done.

The Sweat Ceremony Continued

The final, or fourth round is for the warrior spirit. This round is to honor all the warriors and veterans from the past and for the warrior within to build strength for each brother's own struggles. At the end of the fourth round they yell, "Aho Mitakuye Oyas'in!"

When the brothers leave the inipi, all who did not sweat and the fire keeper are waiting in a line in front of the fence surrounding the religious grounds. They shake hands as those who participated inside, exit and stand in a line. The conductor is the last one to exit the inipi and shakes everyone's hand then stands at the end of the line. All the Native inmates place their hands up in the air and the conductor says one last prayer, which ends with everyone saying, "Aho Mitakuye Oyos'in!" one last time.

Occasionally, an extra round called a buffalo round is performed. It is conducted for a special occasion, for special prayers or because the rocks still have *energy* and enough for everyone to enjoy another round.

During the ceremony many prayers are spoken and songs are sung. The songs are sung for healing, prayer and to honor those who have moved on to the spirit world. After the ceremony, the brothers know that the prayers have been heard by the Creator. Once the ceremony is finished, the participants are spiritually cleansed and ready to start a new week.

Storing the Sweat Lodge Items in Prison

Once the rounds have concluded and the brothers have exited the sweat lodge, the inipi is disassembled. The blankets covering the inipi are removed and placed in large laundry bags. All the tools used in the ceremony are cleaned off and placed on a cart to return to storage. Meanwhile, brothers wash off and prepare to return to their cell. Everyone ensures that everything in the area is cleaned up. Brothers return the shovel, rake and hose to the location where the officers store them. The blankets go to the laundry. The sacred pipe and large drum are stored in a locked closet in the chaplain's office.

The following items are kept in the chaplain's office or in the Native American's religious box: sacred pipe, Pow Wow drum, hand drum, kettle drum, gourd rattles and other religious instruments. Personal items are usually brought to the ceremony in a religious box. Items may include abalone shell, herbs for smudging, tobacco and tobacco mix, feather, headband, religious necklace or choker necklace, corn husks or rolling papers and other religious items vital to the Native's specific beliefs. Items kept in a religious box vary by Tribe.

Prison Hindrances in Holding Sweat Ceremonies

Thanks to the Native relations who held onto their beliefs, Native American inmates can conduct and continue their traditions today. The recordings of elders like Black Elk, the teachings of Leonard Crow Dog for the American Indian Movement, the advocacy of leaders like Len Foster and Walter Echo-Hawk, the Native American Brotherhood (NAB) and all who stood and stand for traditional Native religious practices have made it possible for inmates today to have sweat lodges in Arizona prisons.

Unfortunately, Native inmates need to be wary that treatment in any prison can change at any time, depending on who is in leadership of the religious department. It can be difficult to set up a sweat lodge, even though there are provisions for it in ADOCs policy. *The prison won't make it easy to get the items necessary to conduct a sweat.*

According to Kisto, the ADOC Manual provides procedural guidelines to security officers on how to properly conduct searches of the sacred ground in order to prevent intentional and unintentional desecration of the sweat lodge area.

> "The most feasible method in which both inmate and institution needs are met involves having security visually inspect religious articles and worship areas in the presence of the Indian inmate (with two at the sweat lodge) and the Chaplain."

CHAPTER 3

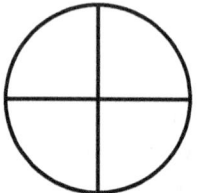

SWEAT LODGE DESECRATION

Many Native American inmates have had their sacred objects desecrated and disrespected at some point during their incarceration. Most Native Americans have also had their religious area desecrated and disrespected in prison. Those who complain about their religious items and area being desecrated have been retaliated against, taken to the hole (administrative segregation) and even shipped to another unit.

ADOC Sweat Lodge Policy

The sweat lodge is susceptible to desecration by officers during searches if Native American religious practitioners aren't present to assist in the search. Rose Ann Kisto wrote in the *ADOC Native American Religious Services Program Manual,*

> "Search of the sweat lodge grounds should take place only when at least two Indian inmates and one Chaplain are present. Because Indian religious practice is protected by federal law, it is important to safeguard the lodge and all Indian worship implements from unintentional and intentional desecration by institution staff. With the Indian inmates and Chaplain present all inquiries and inspections can take place without incident."

On June 11, 2006, the policy read: DO 900/904, 4.4.1.9

> Sweat Lodge sites and all associated storage areas are subject to search. As sweat lodges and fire pits are sacred

areas, searches shall be conducted with prior approval from Shift Commanders and appropriate notification of Wardens or Deputy Wardens and Chaplains.

Many Native American inmates believe that the current policy is inadequate to protect Native American sacred objects and the sacred area. The officers and chaplain are not given any guidelines on how to identify a sacred object and how to properly handle and treat the object with respect.

Examples of Desecration

Negativity

The area in which the sweat lodge is placed carries an energy that increases as prayer continues. This energy can be corrupted by disrespectful actions and by certain things which contradict the energy. Native American religious practitioners believe that un-pure people should stay out of the lodge unless they can clear their negative thoughts. This means that people with low moral standards should stay out of the sweat lodge area, especially if the person is perceived to be a carrier of a negative *aura*. ***Although this view may seem subjective, Native Americans do not ask that others share their beliefs, but that their beliefs are respected.***

Moontime

The Federal Bureau of Prisons Inmate Religious Beliefs and Practices states,

> "Native Americans prohibit women from handling the pipe, or nearing the sweat lodge during menstruation, because they believe that her menstruation-related energy overpowers the power of the sacred object."

Female officers and the chaplain should be made aware of Native American moontime traditional beliefs, otherwise, a female officer has the potential to desecrate sacred objects.

There are certain rules that must be followed. Black Elk, in the book *The Sacred Pipe* stated,

"… she should know, further that each month when her period arrives, she bears influence with which she must be careful, for the presence of a woman in this condition may take away the power of a holy man."

CHAPTER 4

ARIZONA DEPARTMENT OF CORRECTIONS (ADOC) AND THE NATIVE AMERICAN SWEAT LODGE

Desecration of a Sweat Lodge

In 2009, at an Arizona Department of Corrections prison, two security officers and the Chaplain desecrated the sweat lodge during a quarterly search when no code of search conduct was followed. During the search, a female officer entered the sweat lodge area, holes were smashed into the sides of the purification chamber, artwork was wiped out on the spiritual grounds and the sacred rocks were touched. The outcome was the desecration and vandalism of the brother's sweat lodge and religious items. The inmates felt that the guards entered the lodge with contempt and negativity on their mind.

Had any of the sweat lodge members been present, none of this would have happened. In the past, one or two Native American inmates were present during the searches. They would be permitted to move the items that had to be searched. It is the chaplain's responsibility to ensure that Native American religious protocol is followed and on this particular day he failed to protect the sacredness of the lodge area and the religious objects. The officers and the Chaplain seemed to invent the search protocol, as no proper chain of evidence was followed. The guards sifted through the sweat lodge area without understanding the necessity to protect its nature, so the physical damage to the sweat lodge was unjustified. There was no need to damage the sweat lodge and dig in the grounds around it.

In front of the lodge area was a twenty foot by ten foot sandy area where Eagle had drawn Native American symbols in the sand. While performing the search with metal detectors, the officers wiped out the religious symbols that were sculpted in the earth in front of the sweat lodge area with their feet in a malicious manner. The officers used a shovel to dig inside and around the sweat lodge area because they said the metal detector was *set off*.

According to Grey Bear, "In prison, correctional officers and inmates communicate about things that prison administrators wish they didn't. One of the officers who watched the search take place, spoke to me and other Native Americans about what transpired. Also, a Native American inmate who worked in the kitchen watched the search being conducted through the window."

The Chaplain who had no knowledge of Native American religious practice, also spoke to the Native American prisoners about the search. When Native American prisoners asked the correctional officers for the metal items found, nothing was produced. When asked why the guards obliterated the artwork symbolizing their culture, no answer was given. One of the correctional officers who witnessed the search told the Native inmates privately that the other officers were joking around on the grounds and the female officer started dancing on the sweat lodge grounds, mocking Native Americans.

Holes were smashed into the side of the purification chamber. A small one-foot tall wall was built around the sweat lodge to help keep in the heat. Correctional officers used shovels to dig several holes in the wall and on the area around the sweat lodge. The officers desecrated the sacred rocks, their ancestors, by touching them. The rocks should only have been touched by the Chaplain, as this is his duty.

Then, without consent from any Native American, a female officer entered the sweat lodge. No Native American inmate was consulted before she entered the premises. She was asked whether she was having her menstrual period (moontime) around the time of the search and it was determined by the Native American prisoners, that that was the case. She should have stayed away from the sweat lodge. It turns out that when she touched and entered the sweat lodge, it became desecrated, causing it to be unusable. If the Chaplain knew that a menstruating female would desecrate the sweat lodge, the situation could have been avoided. *Note:* Females are allowed to enter some sweat lodges, but not others, depending on the beliefs of the practitioners.

After learning about the events that occurred, the approximately fifty Native American prisoners contemplated retaliating against the Chaplain and correctional officers. All options were put on the table in a series of discussions. One of the proposed responses was to smash all the windows of the multi-faith room (prison chapel). Other options included violence which would lead to a lot of brothers being segregated and removed from the yard as a result. There were some who wanted to retaliate against the female officer and others who wanted to retaliate against the Chaplain.

Grey Bear explains, "Still new on the prison yard, I adopted the role of liaison between the Native American prisoners and the Chaplain and stepped forward into the center of this controversy to prevent my fellow brothers from starting a riot. At the next circle I spoke up in a loud voice, 'I know what to do!' My option was to file grievances to prison administration. The grievances would go up the entire chain of command, starting with the Chaplain, then up to the Warden, then to the Pastoral Activities Administrator, and finally to the Director of the Arizona Department of Corrections."

Officers took photographic evidence of the damage to the sweat lodge only after the inmates requested photos be taken. When the brothers asked for copies of the photos, none were produced, so it is unknown if the pictures were saved as documentation. The Lieutenant stated at the time that an Information Report (IR) would be conducted.

Grey Bear states, "The worst part of the entire event was the state of minds of the officers. They joked and danced on the sweat lodge area and their behavior was disrespectful. In my opinion, they spread this state of mind onto what little we had, our religious values and our dignity. The brother's complaints indicated the correctional staff's indifference to our beliefs and emotions."

One officer was known to be a very disrespectful person and mistreated inmates. If the Native American prisoners had a say in it, this officer would have never been allowed to enter the sweat lodge grounds. Predictably, it was the same officer who started dancing next to the sweat lodge during the search.

The Saturday following the incident, the Chaplain and Lieutenant addressed the inmates at the sweat lodge area. The Chaplain admitted that he was new to the position and stated that he did not have much knowledge of Native American religion, but he was learning on his own time. He indicated that he did not want to be involved in taking an inventory of the religious items, because he *did not have the proper training.* The guards also did not have the proper training, permission and respectful state of mind to do so.

Since the Chaplain did not have a clue regarding Native American beliefs and his role in handling the sacred items, he was unable to protect them. The Lieutenant indicated that he was not present at the time of the search but made the statement that the search could have been conducted in a better manner. At the time, the Lieutenant had been one of the few high-ranking officers who had shown any empathy for the situation. He indicated he would write an IR about the incident.

So, the sweat lodge was laid to rest by dismantling it. The willows were given back to Mother Earth and Father Sky. The Native brothers continued to sing, pray and smudge every Saturday, but there were difficulties. After the grievances about the sweat lodge desecration were filed, prison officials retaliated by reducing the inmates time for ceremonies, removing the water drum and blocking the use of the sweat lodge grounds for talking circles. When told to have their weekly talking circles in the multi-faith room, all the Native American prisoners refused. Instead, against the prison Chaplain's wishes, they held them outside on Mother Earth and stood their ground for their beliefs.

Grievances

The Native American beliefs were shared with many members of the administration through letters, also known as *kites* every time a violation occurred. There were several Native Americans on Grey Bear's yard who would send kites to the religious administration. There were around a dozen kites sent; however, those letters seemed to have disappeared. Staff would not admit that they received them and did not place the information in the chaplain's office, where they were supposed to be kept.

The first of several grievances over the discriminative treatment of the Native American group by prison officials was filed shortly after the incident. After a year of grievances and several conversations with officials, Grey Bear was able to understand the general opinion of Arizona's prison officials as it related to the Native American religious rights.

First, the grievances they submitted were returned with a *big red NO* stamp denying relief to their issues, quoting that ADOC was following policy as it was written. Then ADOC simply avoided responding to any issues brought up concerning Native American religious practice. Grey Bear found himself in the chaplain's and prison supervisor's office several times; and sometimes the prison warden was there to discuss these issues with him. Grey Bear told the ADOC Administration that they were violating Native American religious rights. They tried to intimidate him, but he still wrote dozens of inmate letters and grievances to expose ADOC for violating their rights. Eventually, every response from ADOC that Grey Bear received was submitted to the US District Court. With no resolution in sight, Grey Bear sued the Arizona Department of Corrections by himself, but on behalf of all his Native brother's religious rights.

Post Incident Report Outcome

Relating to grievances from May 2009 regarding the sweat lodge issues, the private prison failed to explain why its officers did not use *appropriate respect* when handling religious items. Instead they retaliated by locking up two of the Native American prisoners' main spiritual representatives. The following day, the prison officials called a meeting with thirteen lodge members and other prison staff to inform the Native brothers that a *memo* prevented them from using the sweat lodge area for anything but sweat ceremonies.

In June 2009, the gates were welded shut on the small fence surrounding the lodge area and the inmates were told to stay out or be penalized by being sent to the hole. At the time, several of them were questioned, threatened and harassed by the correctional officers. Inmates were summoned individually and interrogated by a high-ranking correctional officer. In mid-June, Eagle, the main spiritual representative and pipe holder who ran the sweats, was sent to the *hole* (administrative segregation). At the beginning of August, the brothers were informed Eagle was sent to another unit.

With the loss of their pipe holder, Walks in Faith, Grey Bear's cousin, became the new pipe holder. He sent an inmate letter to the Chaplain and prison administration requesting an additional drum. As a result of his inmate letter, the Chaplain was told by his superior to throw away the only instrument they had, the kettle drum. Their sacred instrument was treated like trash by the administration. For months the Native inmates were without any musical instruments for their ceremony, and because of this action, they decided to stand up for their people.

CHAPTER 5

RELIGIOUS RIGHT TO HAVE A SWEAT LODGE IN PRISON

Laws Passed for American Indian Religious Freedom

In 1978, the 95th Congress passed public law 95-341. The official resolution is called the *American Indian Religious Freedom Act* (AIRFA). Part of it states,

> "... it shall be the policy of the United States of America to protect and preserve for American Indians their inherent right of freedom to believe, express and exercise the traditional religions of the American Indian, Eskimo, Aleut and Native Hawaiians, including but not limited to access to sites, use and possession of sacred objects, and the freedom to worship through ceremonials and traditional rites."

There are no specific guidelines or provisions for enforcement written in the Act. The Act does little to protect American Indian rights in court for civil actions. AIRFA has no teeth to bite with when Native Americans tried to use the act in court cases. It failed to provide remedy.

The Religious Land Use and Institutionalized Persons Act (RLUIPA) was passed by Congress in 2000. This law benefited prisoners by giving them a method to stand up for their rights. The prison cannot cause a substantial burden to religious exercise without good cause. RLUIPA provides that:

"No government shall impose a substantial burden on the religious exercise of a person..." unless the government establishes that the burden furthers "a compelling governmental interest," and does so by "the least restrictive means." 42 U.S.C. §2000cc-1(a) (1)-(2).

Religious Rights and Court Cases/Prison Manuals

This section is written in legal style and references court cases that back up the statements and quotes that were used in the court case and were central to this book.

In 1992, the Federal Bureau of Prisons created a guidebook titled, *American Indian Spirituality: Beliefs and Practices*. Federal guidelines only pertain to Federal prisons; states can use them as guidelines for their own statutes or ignore them completely.

A document named *The Arizona Department of Corrections (ADOC), Native American Religious Services Program Manual* (revised 1994), states on page sixteen that the sweat lodge ceremony frequency is at least once per week and "may be in addition to or in substitution of the talking circle". This statement was used in the ADOC policy in 1994, but was modified so the word *shall* was changed to *may* i.e. ADOC Policy 900/904 "1.4.1.2.1 ceremonies may be held on a weekly basis . . .". This wording softens the requirement.

In the case, Allen v. Toombs, 827 F.2d (9th Cir. 1987) which took place at the Oregon State Penitentiary in 1987, the following statement was made:

> "The sacred sweat lodge ritual takes place in a small hut-like structure built from willows and blankets. Large rocks are heated in a fire pit outside the lodge, and then by means of a pitchfork, are placed in the lodge, where water is poured over them to create steam. Herbs are burned for purification. Participants enter the lodge naked, to pray and meditate, and to purge the body and the spirit. The ceremony lasts between one and one-half hours to two hours."

Another case at the Oregon State Penitentiary (OSP) states,

> "a sweat lodge and adjoining fire pit have been built in the industrial area of the prison for the use of inmates in the general prison population. The ceremony is held weekly on Saturday." In Reinert v. Haas, the lodge was, "an absolutely essential part of worship."

How often should sweat ceremonies be held? Arizona Revised Statute 31-206(b) states,

> "The Chaplain shall hold services at the state prison at least twice each month."

The US Department of Justice, Federal Bureau of Prisons, *Inmate Religious Beliefs atrnd Practices Technical Reference Manual* states,

> "a sweat lodge is typically used once each week, but may be operated more frequently as the program requirements of the Chaplaincy Department and institution allows. The Chaplain may request approval for additional use of the sweat lodge in cases where an individual expresses special needs. Inmates may often request to observe national holidays, deaths, and the seasonal equinox or solstice with a sweat lodge ceremony".

The manual also states,

> "Further, talking circles, other educational opportunities, or ceremonial song/drum practices are allowed weekly as time and space permit".

The prison cannot engage in *interference with a tenet or belief that is central* to one's religion (see Bryant v. Gomez, 46 F.3d 948, 949, (9th Cir. 1995).) Courts in Thomas v. Gunter, 1994, allowed weekend and holiday access to the sweat lodge. For courts in Thomas v. Gunter, 1997, the court permitted lodge access two to five times weekly, while denying daily access. This is a lot more access than Native American's are allowed in Arizona's prisons.

Prison Grievances Written by Grey Bear

Over the years, Grey Bear wrote inmate letters to officials, gathering up paperwork in order to *prove* what was happening inside Arizona prisons. It is one thing to complain about a situation and how *terrible* things are; but to prove a point takes a tremendous amount of writing and legwork. In order to prove oppression, one must be oppressed. So, for all the wrong reasons, Grey Bear thanked the prison officials (figuratively, not literally) for showing him exactly how their system works.

In October 2010, Grey Bear wrote six separate inmate letters to the Senior Chaplain and mailed them to his office. The issues and answers from the Senior Chaplain are presented in various parts of this book. The final issue, the *checkmate* enacted by the prison system against Native American prisoners was regarding the sweat ceremony. He wrote to the Senior Chaplain stating,

> "Currently, we have no available supply of wood for our sweat ceremony. The sweat ceremony is the main way we gather every week for spiritual purification. A talking circle is not a valid substitute for a sweat ceremony.
>
> A lack of provision for wood in policy causes a substantial burden to the Native American religion. If wood cannot be provided for us, then we should be allowed to have a means to raise funds to buy wood. Depending on outside sponsors to provide wood for us is inadequate to get enough wood on a consistent basis. How are the incarcerated Natives supposed to get wood?"

The Senior Chaplain wrote back,

> "The ADC and private prisons make time and space available for religious ceremony but neither is required to provide ceremonial supplies for any religion. However, donations can be accepted for group ceremonies if they are offered. Fundraising activities do not fall under the authority of this office, but you should be advised that fundraising activities for a specific religious group or activity is not authorized."

Two announcements were posted on the chaplain's window announcing that the prison would not help us gather wood. It stated:

> *October 19, 2010.*
> *To: M. Cruz.*
> *From: Warden.*
> *RE: Sweat Lodge Wood.*
>
> *Chaplain, please ensure that the following is shared with the Native American inmates and that it is posted in your area. Effective November 30, 2010, CACF will no longer be able to allow utilization of the wood supply currently being used for sweat lodge ceremonies. It is our responsibility to ensure that the sweat lodge area is erected and accessible so that inmates are able to conduct sweats as part of the practice of their faith. Donations of wood for use in the sweat lodge will be permitted and any donations will need to be coordinated with CPS.*

The memo barred the Native inmates from using recycled pallets for the fire in the sweat lodge ceremony. So, the Warden stepped in and canceled access to this source. The brothers talked about these issues in a talking circle. First, the brothers had to figure out ways in which they could get wood. Also, it was decided that it would be good to have a group account to gather money to buy wood. Because wood was required for the ceremony, they needed to have options to be self-sufficient. Grey Bear wrote a kite with some questions and included a proposal to the Programs Supervisor.

The note stated:

> *Lumber issue. Our group, the Native American Faith Group is very concerned that we will have difficulty finding sponsorship for wood to use during the sweat lodge ceremony. Depending on outside sponsors is unfeasible. Therefore, we have several important questions that need to be answered:*
>
> • *Are we allowed to purchase wood ourselves?*

> - *Can we pay for the wood and have it delivered?*
>
> - *Can our family members donate wood? If so, what is the paperwork needed? If no, on any of the above questions, why not?*
>
> - *When we get wood, is it going to be divided with another unit?*
>
> - *How much wood is allowed to be donated and will there be a place to store it? (one cord of wood is 4' x 4 x 8')*
>
> - *Can we locate a nearby business and set up an account with it so that wood may be purchased and delivered by the company? If so, what is the paperwork we need? If not, why not?*
>
> *Thank you for help in coordinating these matters.*

On the second kite Grey Bear wrote,

> *I am writing on behalf of the Native American Faith Group. Our group expresses the desire to reach a formal arrangement for the procurement of wood for our sweat ceremony. We propose that an account be set up for the purchase of wood. This account can be donated to by group members. Either the chaplain, program coordinator, or the CPS, is to be in charge of the account and all donations will remain anonymous. When enough money is obtained for the purchase of wood, arrangements will be made, with approval from the Coordinator and Warden, to purchase and have the wood delivered.*
>
> *The Native American Faith Group will work at finding a company that may do this or may try to have an outside sponsor help with this process. This proposal is a preliminary plan to ease the burden of procuring wood with the approval of security, the Warden, and the religious department.*

> *Please let us know what type of arrangements might need to be made to modify this proposal, if any.*
>
> *Approval/Denied: By _____*
> *Comments: _____*

When Grey Bear first submitted the grievance regarding the firewood issues, he argued with the CPO III counselor about the difficulties obtaining firewood for the sweat ceremony. He had similar discussions with other counselors and officials concerning procuring firewood. The result of these discussions always said the same thing,

> "…Why should you Native American even have a sweat lodge? We're not going to build a separate chapel for the other groups!"

Grey Bear's answer,

> "The Native Americans have had sweat lodges long before the Christians had their chapels or Bibles. We refuse to use the *multi-denominational* Christian chapel because you can't build a sweat lodge inside a building. Also, the first thing you see when you walk in the chapel is a bookshelf of Christian publications. There is nothing on it about other religions, how *multi-denominational* is that?"

CHAPTER 6

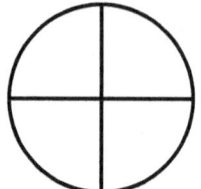

RESOLUTION OF THE ARIZONA DEPARTMENT OF CORRECTIONS OPPRESSION

Concerns as Presented by Grey Bear

Native Americans are a federally protected group. Through the entire process, the Native American inmates were seeking respect and sensitivity for their religious beliefs. The sanctity of their religious sites and sacred items had been overlooked. The inmates felt that a Native American or an officer specifically trained in spiritual respect for Native traditions should be designated to search the sweat lodge area, sweat lodge, altar, fire pit and artifacts.

They also experienced a lack of respect when it came to the searching and handling of their Native American sacred items and religious boxes. Eagle feathers, headbands, herbs, gourds and medicine bags are all considered sacred. The integrity of their faith depends on the care given to these items. It is considered *bad medicine* to allow outsiders to handle them. In the past, officers had the inmates empty the contents of their religious box until the officer was satisfied everything met prison protocol; at no time did they handle or touch the items.

Grey Bear was introduced to religious discrimination when he moved into the same prison dorm as his cousin, Walks in Faith. During a prison unit search, Walks in Faith requested that he be present when a correctional officer wanted to search the sacred items in his religious box. The supervisor came over and said, "We can do whatever we want to your religious box!" At that point, the Native inmates were removed from the building while the officers dumped out the contents of his box onto his bed and left them there when they finished the search. This was considered desecration of his religious objects. Other Native American inmates at the prison unit had similar experiences with their religious boxes and also noticed that the contents of their medicine bag necklaces had been removed during searches.

The Native Americans have faith in their beliefs and Creator. They demanded respect for their religious values and sacred land. The Native Americans were backed into a corner by the refusal of the Administration to accept or validate their religious rights. For every action there is a reaction. The brothers choose to act in a civil manner and they believed that due process was the answer.

The brothers had no objections to being searched, but the way in which the search was conducted was offensive. They requested that respect be shown to the sacred objects and items. A code of conduct stating what is appropriate respect for sacred objectives was needed to be included in prison policy.

GREY BEAR STANDS UP

Below is the proposal I sent to the prison Chaplain, Warden and Pastoral Activities Administration after the sweat lodge was desecrated by correctional officers. The inmates requested that Native American staff members or inmates observe and assist in the searches of the sacred areas. Or at a minimum, a staff member who truly respected our beliefs, faith and all that we hold sacred be present.

The suggested solutions included:

> 1. Code of Conduct Policy needs to be written to protect and define *sacred* objects and *appropriate respect* related to officer behavior.
>
> 2. Standard of Ethics: A reference needs to be set as a foundation of Native American beliefs.
>
> 3. Training: Sensitivity training for officers needs to be required for religious rights.
>
> 4. Herbs: Restrictions on herbs needs to be removed or modified.
>
> 5. Fence: The fence needs to be upgraded to ensure protection and privacy of the sweat lodge area.
>
> 6. Shower: We require an outdoor shower for the sweat lodge area to protect us from heat stroke.
>
> 7. Access: We require access to our sweat lodge area for talking circles and personal smudges.

8. Spiritual Advisor: Provisions and financial compensation needs to be made for an outside spiritual advisor to attend religious ceremonies.

9. Race: Racial restrictions to sweat lodge membership must be abolished at the discretion of the sweat lodge members.

10. Choker and Headband: The traditional choker necklace should be allowed to be purchased and donated from approved vendor(s) and both the choker and headband be allowed to be worn anytime.

11. Memo: Any memo written to restrict the religious rights of inmates should be abolished.

12. Native Holiday: Native holiday food should be accommodated equal to other races.

13. Music Program: The music program should not have the requirement of attending religious services. If so, it should be equal to all religions.

Unless policy changed to protect Native American religious practices and allowed for self-sufficiency, the Native American inmates would continue to suffer from the repeated abuse at the hands of an oppressive bureaucracy.

When problems with religious matters occur in prison, a certain process must be followed in order to enlist change. First, identify the problem. Try not to assume any facts, instead dig for them by asking questions. Second, establish communication with the officials involved. Third, an effort should be made to find reasonable solutions and alternatives for the situation. Fourth, present the problem and propose a solution to officials in a respectful manner. How each issue is approached should be decided on a case by case basis.

If a situation isn't solved through the informal process then the options are: A) let it go, or B) file paperwork. If the brothers decided to let the situation go unresolved, then their rights would be violated by the system and destined to repeat themselves and become even worse. After much consultation with the pipe holder, I decided to file paperwork by submitting a grievance and following through on it.

This also meant filing a civil action in court. Unfortunately, Native Americans have become so accustomed to being oppressed that few (as seen in court cases) have stepped forward to make a change. If a situation cannot be changed, then we as Native Americans are challenged to change ourselves.

The Fourteenth Amendment guarantees equal protection of our rights under the law. *The Jailhouse Lawyer's Handbook* states,

> "A prison cannot make special rules or give special benefits to member(s) of only one religion or group of religions without a reason."

From personal experience as a Native American in prison, my brothers and I would ask weeks in advance to conduct a sweat ceremony during a holiday, only to be denied at the last minute due to *staffing concerns*. We asked for smudges, talking circles and access to a classroom for teaching opportunities, but were denied and no reason given. On one occasion, we were approved to have a smudge on New Year's, but when the time came to hold the ceremony, the security officers broke it up because *no one informed them*.

Miscommunication, ignorance and indifference do not justify religious oppression. Even though a group of inmates may be seen by officers as a security risk, the risk does not justify banning group services if that is the only way to conduct meaningful religious services. See Whitney v. Brown, 882 F.2d 1068 (6th Circ. 1989).

In my experience, prison officials in Arizona actively oppress Native American religious worship in prison. It is difficult to explain to the officials why the ceremonies and practices are so important since the ADOC refuses to acknowledge the Native American beliefs. Religious opportunities for the Native Americans should be equal to that of other religions.

One way to communicate the religious needs of Native American practitioners to non-Indians is to explain to them in terms that they can understand. The Native American sweat lodge is as important to Native Americans, as is a Christian's weekly Sunday service. The Native American group only had one turnout on Saturday and it was denied. The talking circle or smudge is as important and enriching as a Bible study. The different ceremonial herbs we use are like different chapters in the Bible, each one has its own special significance.

In the past, there were written provisions on how searches should be conducted without conflict. Policy was removed and changed in ways that resulted in the desecration of our sacred items. History repeats itself. The refusal of the Administration to correct policy and admit to no wrong-doing is a substantial burden on the Native Americans Free Exercise of Religion.

The goal of the brothers was to come together as a group, united on the Red Road. The path wouldn't be a lonely one, as long as they walked together.

Pathway Toward Redemption

The misunderstanding of other people's beliefs and values is the main cause of conflict in prison, as well as throughout history. There needs to be reasonable rules and explanations for Native American beliefs written into policy to include the meaning of *sacred* and what is considered *appropriate* behavior around sacred areas. Otherwise, anyone can twist the definition to fit their own needs.

All the issues mentioned have been brought up repeatedly in the US Court System. Native Americans want to be able to practice their religion peaceably and hope that prison staff will meet with us as equal human beings and work out a mediation agreement to ensure our religious rights now and in the future. Only with education and open dialogue will future conflict be prevented.

Native American history shows us that not only does oppression occur today in prison, but also to non-incarcerated Natives. The oppression of Native Americans began when *outsiders* came to the Americas. Christopher Columbus was the first warden recorded to enslave and imprison Native Americans. A lot has been written about Native American oppression and these books serve to document history. This book will show the pathway from the Vikings to the current prison environment for Native American prisoners and leads the reader to an environment ready for change and includes a proposal for how it can be acheived.

NATIVE AMERICAN HISTORY

THE FIRST PEOPLES
By Walks in Faith

It has been a long and difficult journey for the Native American – forced removal and relocation from our ancestral lands, hunting grounds and villages; intentional subjection to famine, disease, slavery, torture, rape and murder; plus the foreign invaders of European and Spanish descent who tried to exterminate our religion and languages. Yet through it all, we resolutely remain.

There is a spirit that is sacred

that thrives within us. In the midst of this current

economic crisis, bitter cold of the winters and scorching

heat of the long summers, we fight through the hunger of an

empty stomach, the thirst of a dry mouth. The withdrawals

of addiction and the isolation of incarceration. The racism of

a hateful world and an unjust government at both the state

and national levels. But sometimes the enemy is much closer

to us. The brutality of domestic violence, verbal, emotional,

physical and sexual abuse, the hardships of broken homes

and the emptiness of abandonment.

Yet through it all, our spirit remains. From behind the prison fence we are blessed with the spirit of our ancestors. To know who we are as a people, where we come from and how much we've suffered. Inside the sweat lodge grounds upon Mother Earth we firmly stand and she welcomes our every footstep.

Our sweat, smudge and pipe ceremonies have been handed down for generations. The lava rocks, drum, medicine bags, eagle feathers, gourds, headbands and herbs have all been blessed by our Medicine Man and have been made forever sacred.

The fire pit, altar and inipi have also been blessed and made to be *wakan* (Lakota language for powerful or sacred). We are now connected to the universe and come to life in the realm of the supernatural before, during and after every ceremony.

We now declare that we will not be denied the right to practice our religion and sacred ceremonies. We will not be denied the respect due towards our religious beliefs, ceremonies, sacred grounds and items.

We are the Native American, the Red Nation.

We are the First Peoples.

CHAPTER 1

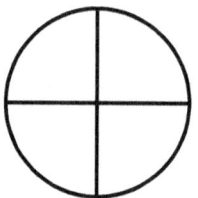

INTRODUCTION

Spotted Owl was an Alaskan Native, a member of the Aleutian Indian tribe. He was asked by Grey Bear to write the introduction to the History section. This is a sampling of the Native American's history.

It is sad when you think about it all – the Native Americans took care of the land and respected the Mother Earth. They only hunted for and used what was needed, leaving no footprint. No one thinks about our religion or culture anymore. I am tired of not saying what's on my mind. It's time to speak up.

According to some books written about American Indians, they state that about 35,000 years ago the first Indian tribe crossed over the ice bridge that covered the Bering Strait Sea into Alaska. The first tribe to cross the ice bridge were the Athapaskan Indians. For many years this tribe lived in Alaska before they spread out to other areas and started other tribes. This hypothesis has been in dispute by scholars.

The Athapaskan's began to migrate south into what is now known as Canada seeking food sources. Others traveled to southern Colorado, Southwestern Kansas, Oklahoma and Texas. By 1350 AD the first Athapaskan's arrived in the southwest. They became known as the Kiowa and Apache Indian tribes, and the Kiowas are connected to the Hopi Indians. The Navajo developed around seven hundred to one-thousand years ago from these groups and live in Utah, New Mexico and Arizona.

There were several migrations that occurred over time and different tribes would adopt the customs of the respective tribes.

After many conflicts with non-natives invading Native American territories, the US government forced many Native American tribes to live on Indian reservations when the Indian Removal Act of 1830 and the Indian Appropriations Act of 1851 were enacted. Whether by Treaty or Executive Order, the reservations were established in natural resource deprived areas and the results were starvation, poverty and poor living conditions for the Natives.

During the 1870s, the government encouraged and often forced the tribal people to cut their hair, dress like White people, adopt the Whites' holidays and give up their traditional religious practices. The children were sent to boarding schools to be reprogrammed to assimilate into White society. The boarding schools were breeding houses for diseases like tuberculosis and many children never returned to their homeland. School officials were known to discourage the students from visiting their family because it would hinder their assimilation into American society. In many cases, children were always forced into manual labor and *forbidden* to practice their spiritual ways; instead they were indoctrinated into Christianity. The boarding school experience was traumatic to the development of Native Americans throughout history.

CHAPTER 2

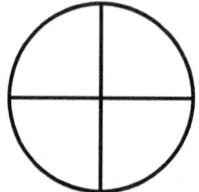

TRIBES OF THE SOUTHWEST AND UNITED STATES OF AMERICA

Introduction

There are many sources of material that discuss the history of Native Americans after their first contact with the Spanish in the United States. This chapter will focus on tribal groups who exist primarily in Arizona and those groups who originated the *Sun Dance Way*, a system of Native American cultural and spiritual religious practices that applies the sweat lodge ceremony style described in this book. These groups include, but are not limited to the Lakota, Cheyenne, Blackfeet and Arapaho, who are part of what is known as the Plains Tribes. The intent is to educate the reader of the context and environment that led to Native American religious oppression in Arizona.

Apache

The Apache bands had originally followed buffalo herds southward and eastward, when they began to raid other tribes and the Spanish. The Apache were many different bands that descended from the Athabascan travelers (Athapaskan and Athabascan are one in the same tribe).

Cochise, Mangas and Nana were three Apache leaders who resisted the government's efforts to place them on reservations in the late 1800s. These men were forced into resistance under pressure from white troops. The white settlers in the region wanted the government to eradicate the Apaches, but the war with the Indians provided economic gain for the whites. The newspapers often ran stories that were one-sided against the Apache and they were often depicted as the aggressor in conflicts. This was common throughout the United States to justify removal.

The Apache had rebelled against the Spanish in 1684 and defied the Americans in what were called the Apache Wars between 1861 and 1890. Cochise and Geronimo were two Apache leaders who resisted the government's efforts to place them on reservations. Geronimo led the last resistance of the Chiricahua in 1884.

One example of the difficulties Native Americans living in the Southwest faced can be recognized in the Aravaipa Apache. Eskiminzin led his band of Apache to Camp Grant to make peace with the government in 1871. While Lieutenant Royal E. Whitman awaited word from the government about what to do with the peaceful Aravaipa, a group of vigilantes attacked the unarmed Aravaipa camp.

Not only did they face hardships from the Mexicans to the south, the Caucasians to the east and from their own Native American neighbors, but a large group of Mexican, White and Tohono O'odham mercenaries killed one-hundred and forty-four of the Aravaipa, many of whom were women and children who were unable to escape. Other bands of Apache heard of this massacre and were subject to the same instigation seen earlier during the Plains Wars.

Some of the perpetrators of the Camp Grant massacre were later tried and acquitted. The head chief of the Aravaipa, Eskiminzin, commented, "The people of Tucson and San Xavier must be crazy. They acted as though they had neither heads nor hearts… they must have a thirst for our blood…These Tucson people write for the papers and tell their own story. The Apaches have no one to tell their story.".

The Quechan and the Mohave

The Quechan and Mohave are two tribes located along the Colorado River in western Arizona. They are related to the Yuman and share a similar language, religious values and beliefs. The Yuman tribe places significant value on dreams as a connection to the spirits and a primary ceremony for these tribes is the cremation ritual after death. Reservations were established in 1865 and by 1895, the Bureau of Indian Affairs forbade the traditional cremation ritual of the Yuman tribes.

North of the Quechan, the Mohave (Aha Macav) used warfare to find glory and honor for themselves and their tribe. They fought against the neighboring Maricopa and Cocopa tribes using war clubs, sticks and bows and arrows. A major part of Mohave spirituality are dreams that tell them about their past, present and future. Dreams told the Mohave about the beginning of all things. Certain Mohave, called Kwanami's, have special, before birth dream powers that enable them to fight spirits.

The Spaniards rarely passed through the Yuman tribes until 1779 when Franciscan missionary Padre Gasces established a mission on the Quechan tribe's homeland (Yuma, AZ). The Quechan did not appreciate the subjugation and killed all the Spanish priests and soldiers. The mission was burned down.

The Yuman tribes had occasional conflicts with the whites when the California gold rush brought them through the Native's land in the 1840s. The Mohaves attacked a wagon train passing through their area in 1858 and the following year the US Government built Fort Mohave and filled it with troops to keep the Indians under watch.

Navajo (Diné)

The Navajo (Diné – meaning *The People*) descended from the Athapascans traveling from the North. The Navajo settled in what is now northeast Arizona, southern Utah and western New Mexico between four sacred mountains; La Plata Mountain to the North (Obsidian Mountain), Mount Taylor to the south (Blue Bead or Turquoise Mountain), San Francisco Peak to the west

(Abalone Shell Mountain) and Blanca Peak to the east (Dawn or White Shell Mountain).

In 1583, Spanish explorers encountered a group of Native Americans north of the Apache. They called them the Apaches de Navajo. Navajo is a Tewa pueblo word which means *cultivated field*. Apache came from the Zuni word *Apachu* which meant *enemy*. The Navajo stayed northwest of the Zuni while the Apache were split into different groups to the southwest, southeast and northeast of the Zuni. The Navajo called themselves Diné while the Apache called themselves the *Tinneh* or *Tinde*, their native names for *the people*.

The Diné developed an agricultural base by copying some of the local pueblo tribes and later added sheep, goats and horses to their livelihood. They are very spiritual and adopted and modified many customs from local tribes. They became adept at making jewelry and weaving amongst many other talents.

The Navajo initially numbered around ten thousand and lived in a stable environment between the sacred mountains until the Spanish came. As of 2015, there were approximately three-hundred thousand enrolled tribal members, but fewer members live on the reservation.

CHAPTER 3

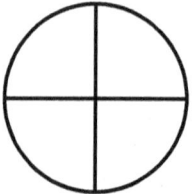

FIRST EUROPEAN CONTACT WITH NATIVE AMERICANS

The Norse

The first Europeans to make contact with Native Americans were the Vikings (Norse) around 1000 AD. The Norse also killed the first Indians they encountered. They attempted to start colonies on the islands around Newfoundland, but bad weather and attacks from the Indians deterred them. The Norse called the Indians *skraelings*, which meant savages, barbarians or screechers.

Christopher Columbus

Christopher Columbus sailed to the New World from Genoa, Italy. Spain paid Columbus to find a direct trade route to Asia. European navigators during the 1400s sought out Asia for its valuable trade goods. He traveled west by sea and *hit* land on October 12, 1492. He thought he was near Japan and always believed he was in Asia throughout his life. He landed on San Salvador, an island he named, in what is now known as the Greater Antilles island group south of the Bahamas. He encountered the peaceful Arawak tribes and because he thought he was in India, he called the people he encountered *Indios* or *Indians*. The Indians welcomed Columbus but were unaware that he had a background of being a slave trader.

Columbus claimed the island for Spain since no Christians had previously claimed it. On June 7, 1494, Spain and

Portugal split up the New World with the Treaty of Tordesillas. This agreement stated that only a *Christian King* would be recognized in the Americas as having any claim to the lands on the American continent. Columbus enslaved and was responsible for the deaths of thousands of the Arawak and ultimately was responsible for the eradication of an entire people.

South of San Salvador, Columbus landed on a large island he named Hispaniola. The island is now known as Haiti and the Dominican Republic. Initially the Indians were friendly to the explorers. On his first trip, Columbus kidnapped six of the Indians and took them back to England to show them off. Most of them died from diseases that they had not ever been exposed to before. When Columbus returned to Hispaniola in 1495, he and his men killed and captured many Indians. Of those he captured, five hundred were shipped to Spain to be sold as slaves.

At one point, Columbus left the island and while he was gone, his men formed into raiding groups. Some joined together to find gold, others attacked local tribes for women and gold. The Indians resisted and killed the plunderers, and when Columbus returned, he found that some of his remaining men had been killed by neighboring tribes. He became a tyrant, a conqueror of the West Indies.

Columbus made many demands from the Indians who survived his wrath. He demanded high taxes of gold, at that time referred to as a *tribute,* from the Indians. They were forced to work on plantations and in gold mines established on the islands by the Spanish. During the 1500s invaders from Spain, Portugal, France and England kidnapped many of the Indians and used them as slaves. Most of the other Indians died from starvation and disease after all the resources on the islands were depleted.

On his third journey to the West Indies, some of Columbus' own men rebelled and formed an alliance with the Indians. Columbus had some of the Spanish men hanged for treason. The monarchy of Spain sent men to overturn Columbus and he was arrested and brought to Spain in chains. Amazingly, Columbus was allowed to return to the islands a fourth time, although he was barred from trespassing onto his former colony. He explored parts of Central America on his fourth journey disrupting Indians as he went.

During the journeys, Columbus and his men used dogs trained to kill people to subdue the Natives. Known as *war dogs,* they were used to hunt the Indians who tried to escape. The captured Indians were tortured in a variety of manners including death by hanging, slowly burned to death, or worse, when the Indian's children were fed to the dogs. The brutality of Columbus is rarely or fully discussed in American history books.

After his final voyage, he suffered from a chronic disease until he passed away in 1506. For three hundred years few people knew who he was or what he did.

Other Europeans Conquer the New World

There were more than eight-hundred thousand different tribes in North America before the European's started arriving. As many as twenty-five to one hundred million Indians once populated the Americas. Once the Europeans started crossing the Atlantic in 1492, they arrived unaware that the land was inhabited. The settlers thought the land was *free for the taking.*

In 1499, an Italian explorer named Amerigo Vespucci came from Portugal to explore the region. Vespucci is credited with naming the American continent the *mundus novus,* or *New World.* He explored islands south of those Columbus discovered and because the land was considered to be undiscovered by Europeans, he called the region the *New World,* ignoring that the Indians already lived there. Vespucci published his findings and eventually gained notoriety for it. Mapmakers named the continent *America* after him (Amerigo).

In 1500, Portuguese explorer Gaspar Corte-Real explored Newfoundland where he encountered the Beothuk Indians, who were friendly. Later, the French and English who settled in Newfoundland killed off the Beothuk Indians.

English explorer John Cabot was the first Englishman to walk on North American soil in Newfoundland. He claimed the land for King Henry the VII, kidnapped three Micmac Indians and took them back to England where he used them as *show and tell* to gain notoriety and more money for further exploration. He disappeared on his second voyage.

Various European countries expressed interest in exploiting the New World for gold, new places to settle and to introduce Christianity to the Indians. Europeans brought many changes to the Americas in the 1500s, but it was Spain that lead the way to death and destruction for the Native American tribes.

Spain

The Spanish settled in Central and South America, Arizona, California, New Mexico, Florida, Texas, Mexico, the Antilles and the Bahama islands. The Spanish brought domestic animals, such as horses and cattle to the New World, as well as diseases that devastated the Indians. The Spanish also enslaved the Natives, forced Christianity, and waged genocide against the Native American people.

The Spanish had recently warred with the Muslims. They killed and conquered for Christianity and gold. In 1513, Spanish explorer Ponce de Leon was the first European to set foot on what is now US soil. He named the area La Florida.

Spanish explorer Hernan Cortes explored Mexico in 1519 and found that the Indians possessed gold. Using advanced weaponry, enemy Indian tribes and assisted by an epidemic of smallpox, his six-hundred soldiers conquered the Aztec. The Native people had never been exposed to many of the diseases that the European conquerors passed to them, so they had no resistance or treatments. The sick and the dead overwhelmed the culture of the indigenous people.

In 1528, Alvar Nunez Cabeza de Vaca became stranded in Florida. He made his way to Mexico, losing three-hundred men and barely surviving himself. His account led other Spanish explorers to believe great riches existed in North America.

Francisco Pizarro was sent and conquered the Inca in South

America in 1530 with a force of one-hundred eighty men and thirty-seven horses. Due to the actions of the Spanish conquistadors, thousands of Indians were killed in the name of progress. Indians in Central America and South America who survived, lived under systems of indentured servitude under Spanish rule.

In 1539, Hernan De Soto marched through east and central North America with six-hundred soldiers. He and his men ravaged their way through Florida, Georgia, the Carolinas, Tennessee, Alabama, Mississippi and Arkansas leaving a trail of burned villages and dead Indians. The largest resistance De Soto's army met was at Mavila, Alabama where De Soto's men massacred twenty-five hundred to three-thousand Indians on October 18, 1550. De Soto's men suffered casualties that demoralized and weakened them. He would take captives to transport the Spanish supplies and use the captive women as sex slaves for his men. After De Soto's men crossed the Mississippi, De Soto died from illness and his men retreated.

In 1540, Spanish conquistador Francisco Vasquez de Coronado invaded Southwestern North America. With over a thousand soldiers, he attacked the Zuni Pueblo. When he found no gold or precious stones as he traveled eastward, Coronado and his men destroyed many pueblos, Indian villages and killed hundreds of captured Indians by burning them alive at the stake. He used his war dogs to attack the natives, as the dogs were bred to kill people. The dogs were also used to kill the leaders of the tribes in an effort to dishearten the Natives, as the conquistadors moved onward.

Coronado and his men raped and pillaged throughout the southwest. They traveled to what is now known as Kansas searching for gold. Coronado returned empty handed to Mexico, where he faced charges from the Spanish crown for excessive brutality against the Indians. He was acquitted. The slaves and porters died from poor treatment and most of the tribes that were attacked never recovered. A wave of disease, especially smallpox, spread through the surviving Indians.

Europeans Settle in the New World

The first illegal immigrants to America were European. The French, Dutch and English established settlements on the East Coast of North America.

In 1585 English colonists under the direction of Sir Walter Raleigh traveled to the area that is now Virginia. Initially, the colonists got along with the friendly Roanoke Tribe. Later, a dispute over a missing silver cup prompted the English to burn down a Roanoke village and all their crops. This led to an escalation of conflicts with the Indians. The Indians then destroyed the English colony nearly killing all the settlers. A second colony was built in the same location and that colony was destroyed as well.

In the 1600s many colonies were established along the East coast of North America. Jamestown (Massachusetts) was founded in 1607 by English settlers. Quebec (Canada) was founded in 1608 by the French and Plymouth (Massachusetts) was founded in 1620.

By 1608, settlers from Jamestown started raiding and killing the Indians. Governor Thomas Gates was ordered by his superiors to indenture the local Indians and demand tribute (taxes) from them. In 1610, Lord De La Warr led Jamestown settlers to massacre local Indians, killing the Sachem female leader and her children in cold blood.

In 1613, colonists started shipping tobacco to England creating a great demand. Slaves, indentured servants and rejects of society started moving to New England and Virginia. During the 17th century, seventy-five percent of the colonies were either slaves or indentured servants of some kind. In 1622, the town of Henricus was destroyed in an Indian uprising led by Opechancanough, brother of Powhatan. Three hundred and fifty colonists were killed, but the remaining colonists fought back causing mass destruction of the local tribes until Opachancanough was defeated in 1644.

In 1637, the Pilgrims sent out a group of men to help participate in the destruction of the Pequot Tribe in Mystic, Connecticut. Known as the Pequot War, over seven hundred Indian men, women and children were killed, and their villages were burned wiping out the tribe. There have been links to this slaughter as a cause for celebration by the Pilgrims which may have led to the basis of Thanksgiving.

Indian tribes were nearly wiped out in the New England and Virginia colonies by disease and conflicts with the colonists. According to Takaki, eighty-five percent of the Indian population, more than fifty-five thousand indigenous people died in southern New England between 1610 and 1675. During King Phillip's War from 1675 to 1676, six thousand Indians are estimated to have died from combat and disease.

The Quakers established a colony in North America, and like the Puritans, the Quakers were treated poorly in England because they held different values than the Protestant Church of England. King Charles II happened to owe a debt to William Penn, a Quaker, who wanted to immigrate to North America. The King gave Penn a land grant in North America to repay the debt and in 1682 William Penn and the Quakers founded Pennsylvania.

William Penn endorsed religious freedom for the colonists. Catholics, Jews and other religions were allowed to be part of the colony. Penn befriended the Indians. He treated the local Lenape Tribe (also called the Delaware Tribe) with great respect. He paid compensation to the Indians for the land and met with the Lenape Chief Tamanend III under the Shackamaxon Elm to establish the Great Treaty between the Lenape and the Quakers. They exchanged a wampum belt and established a peace that would last fifty years.

After Penn passed away, his successors betrayed the Lenape with a new treaty called the Walking Purchase and the Lenape were treated as a menace, along with other tribes and colonies throughout the east. The Lenape were eventually ripped away from their homeland by the white settlers in the 1800s. The Delaware Tribe was moved from different reservations causing much hardship. By 1868 they had been moved from Pennsylvania, to Indiana, Ohio, Missouri, Kansas, then finally to Oklahoma by horse and foot.

From 1817 through the 1880s, forty-two Indian tribes were relocated to Oklahoma. Europeans kept pushing the Native Americans further west. During this time over forty-five thousand Indian men, women and children were killed. By the 1900s the Native American population was reduced to two hundred fifty thousand due to diseases brought by the Europeans, starvation from placement on reservations and genocide caused by the active extermination of Native American tribal nations by European occupation. The Europeans nearly destroyed all the Indians of North America.

Genocidal practices have been repeated countless times as Native Americans were pushed further and further west through the use of force. Many reservations were nothing more than concentration camps where many died from disease and starvation. After the Indian Removal Act of 1830 was signed by President Andrew Jackson and enacted, the government removed over seventeen thousand Cherokee from their ancestral homeland. The Natives were placed in stockades, then forcibly marched one hundred and twenty miles to a reservation. Over four thousand Cherokee died during the Trail of Tears in 1838-1839; while forty different tribes were forced to relocate to Oklahoma. Indian tribes in the east were relocated to the west at gunpoint by the federal troops.

Native Americans in all states lived with active oppression of their religion on reservations. Native American tribes on reservations across the United States were discouraged from their religious practice by the anti-Indian laws at the time.

In 1883, the Commissioner of Indian Affairs recommended to Congress that Native American religious practice should be outlawed and created *The Court of Indian Offenses* and made the spiritual activities of medicine men illegal, with the penalty that they *shall be confined in the agency prison for a term not less than ten days.* In 1884 *pagan* American Indian ceremonial practice became illegal, with a penalty of thirty days imprisonment and other penalties. It wasn't until 1930 when the government eased the restrictions for the Pueblo's, but other tribes waited until 1978.

CHAPTER 4

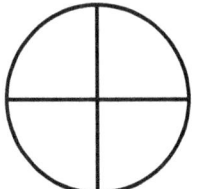

SOUTHWEST TRIBES AND THE US GOVERNMENT

The Civil War and President Lincoln

From 1861 to 1865 the Civil War preoccupied President Abraham Lincoln's concerns, and Native Americans were considered a nuisance to the European colonization of the United States at this time. The issue of slavery was a major cause of the Civil War. Native Americans participated in some of the battles that occurred, taking either the Union or Confederacy side. In 1862 Lincoln intervened in what was called the Sioux Uprising in Minnesota. The government had fallen short into disbursing its treaty obligations to the Sioux and withheld food rations from them.

As a result, the Sioux were starving and dying. The Sioux Uprising broke out resulting in a thirty-seven-day war that led to the deaths of five-hundred Americans and thirty-eight Sioux Indians. After the conflict, three-hundred and three of the Native Americans were sentenced to death. Lincoln intervened by commuting the death sentences of most of the Sioux prisoners, but authorized the execution of thirty-eight of them, *the largest mass execution in American history.* President Lincoln showed he tried to make peace with some of the tribes during this period by giving the Cheyenne and Arapaho Tribes American flags as a gesture of peace. But the atrocities and massacres committed by the Third Colorado Calvary and Colonel John Chivington would undermine this truce.

Native Land and the Government

In Colorado during 1862, government troops started randomly attacking the Cheyenne and Arapaho people and villages. The Indians did nothing to provoke the attacks and the American soldiers indiscriminately killed women, children and infants. At the heart of the carnage was a former Methodist preacher, Colonel John M. Chivington. Chivington preached to his troops that all Indians were heathens and deserved to be wiped out. Chivington said the children and infants should also be killed because *nits make lice.*

In November 1864, Colonel Chivington's troops surrounded an undefended Cheyenne camp of mostly women, children and elders, while the men of the camp had gone hunting for food. According to Brown, the soldiers opened fire with impunity and one hundred and eight women and children died while twenty-eight men were killed. The soldiers mutilated the bodies of the dead Indians by scalping them, cutting off their genitals and other parts of the dead Indians, displaying the parts as trophies.

When the men returned from hunting and gathering food for their people, they found the women, children and elders all dead. This is called the massacre of Sand Creek. Once the word had spread about what happened, warriors came from the plains to join in brotherhood. The Sioux, Cheyenne and Arapaho smoked their pipes dedicated to war. At the beginning of 1865, thousands of Indians fought for what little they had left. They attacked settlements, forts and wagons in guerilla style warfare. They faced impossible odds, yet always remained brave.

In 1866, the Indian alliance was able to defeat eighty-one soldiers in an attack called Fetterman's Massacre. It should be noted that the Whites called the massacres of Indian women and children *battles,* but when armed US soldiers were killed it was called a *massacre*. Other tribes like the Paiutes and Piegan Blackfeet suffered similar massacres by government troops. The goal of the government was to exterminate or force the Indians to cede their land.

Many warriors of the plains would stand up against the US

government. Roman Nose of the Southern Cheyenne, Red Cloud of the Oglala Dakotas, Hump of the Miniconjou, and Sitting Bull and Crazy Horse of the Oglala were some of the Indian leaders who tried to defend the plains from white incursion. The Kiowa and the Comanche Tribes also joined the alliance.

The advanced weaponry of the government troops and the endless stream of US soldiers would eventually overwhelm the Indian alliance, forcing most tribes throughout the United States to sign away their land with treaties.

The US Government

The 1800s were the years of massacres and battles leading to the submission of the Indian tribes in America. The US military developed new ways to kill people with repeating rifles and explosive cannons. The government had designed systems for mass incarceration that would be used on the Indians and later in society. On the reservations, traders cheated the Indians while government agents joined in or looked the other way. Many Indians starved to death. Traders introduced alcohol to the reservations.

Eventually the relentless might of government forces would overcome the heroic efforts of the American Indians. The Sioux signed a treaty in 1868 to end the bloodshed. In 1872, the government came up with a new way to decimate the Indians through environmental warfare, by killing all the buffalo.

In March 1876 government troops once again attacked a camp of Oglala Sioux and Cheyenne Indians without provocation. The soldiers burned the camp and released the Indian's horses.

Many of the Indians escaped and made their way to Crazy Horse's nearby camp. It was at the camp of Crazy Horse that the Sioux decided to go to war again. Crazy Horse and Sitting Bull of the Oglala Sioux were joined by other tribes and were able to defeat Colonel George Armstrong Custer at the Battle of Little Bighorn in June 25, 1876.

After this, the Plains Indians were eventually defeated and Sitting Bull and Crazy Horse went into hiding. Crazy Horse was captured by Little Big Man, who had fought by his side in the past.

Crazy Horse was killed while being detained. His parents buried his body in a secret location near Wounded Knee Creek. Spotted Tail and Red Cloud were coerced to sign away the Black Hills in 1877. Sitting Bull escaped to Canada with a group of his followers, then returned to the Sioux reservation in 1881.

It was during this time that Crow Dog killed Spotted Tail. They were both Lakota leaders who had conflicts with each other. Crow Dog was sentenced to be hanged for the killing, but the Supreme Court overturned the ruling. The backlash from Congress resulted in the Major Crimes Act of 1885, giving Federal Courts jurisdiction over major crimes on Indian reservations.

Navajo and the US Government

In 1773, a Navajo boy named Narbona was seven years old when the Utes started raiding the Navajo homeland. They killed the men, scared away the livestock and destroyed the fields. According to Lapahie, the Utes captured the women and children who were sold as slaves to the Spaniards in New Mexico. A skilled warrior and leader, Narbona grew up fighting and raiding the Spanish, Pueblo and Ute settlements.

In 1805, a temporary treaty was signed for peace; however, more conflicts happened with the Comanche and Spanish until another treaty was signed in 1819. This treaty and another signed in 1823 had little effect, as many raids occurred and many Navajo were captured. After the US troops arrived in the southwest in 1846, Narbona traveled to Santa Fe, New Mexico, to see the American forces camped close by. From a mountain, he could see that the Diné could never overtake the US Army forces. US troops instigated conflict with the Navajo by entering into areas they farmed, scaring and killing their livestock, and burning their fields.

On August 31, 1849, Narbona, along with hundreds of warriors by his side, met with US Lieutenant John M. Washington to start the peace process. He led the process between the Navajo and the United Sates and worked on having several treaties signed, but they were never ratified by Congress.

After making concessions in the treaty, there was a dispute between the Navajo and the white soldiers. A US soldier claimed that one of the Navajo's horses belonged to him and that it had been stolen from him. When the soldiers went to claim the horse, the Navajos started to run away. Washington ordered his men to fire their rifles and cannon at the Navajo. Narbona was one of the many shot and killed that day. He wanted to quell the aggression and sacrificed his life for peace. In September 1849, the first treaty with the Navajo was ratified by Congress.

Gold, Land and Natural Resources

Between 1632 and 1890 the United States government wrote around four hundred treaties and failed to honor every one of them. Chief Red Cloud of the Sioux once said, "They make us many promises, more than I can remember...they never kept but one: they promised to take our land and they took it!" All the Native Americans who survived, were placed on reservations.

In 1850, the US constructed Fort Defiance in the middle of Navajo country. Conflict built up and in 1860 the son-in-law of Narbona, Manuelito, allied with Barboncito and led an attack on Fort Defiance. In 1862, Brigadier General James Carleton planned to relocate the Navajo to Fort Sumner in New Mexico to gain access to Navajo land which he hoped contained gold.

The prior treaty was ignored by government agents in charge of the area. Conflicts erupted between the Navajo and whites. In 1863, US Army Colonel Kit Carson waged a campaign to destroy the Navajo homeland and kill and starve its inhabitants. Under the ruthless orders of Brigadier General James Carleton, Kit Carson's men marched through Canyon de Chelly burning corn and peach fields, killing livestock, spoiling wells and randomly killing Navajos without provocation.

When natural resources such as oil, coal and uranium were found on Native American land, corporations sought to remove the people who lived there. The discovery of natural resources on the Navajo reservation led to tribal revenues and controversy that resulted in the strengthening of the Navajo Nation Tribal Council in the 1920s. Other tribes were not so fortunate. The *termination period* was a time during the 1950s when Congress sought to pass acts in order to end Indian reservations and remove political power from Native Americans. Also, during the termination period, corporations began to *discover* natural resources on Native American reservations. Years earlier the government and corporations conspired to take away the Indian land for gold, now they would go after oil, gas and uranium.

Gold on the west coast prompted the California gold rush in the 1840s. Tribes along the western coast were forced to submit to the government reservation system and suffered a similar fate as the tribes in the East. In 1849, the California gold rush caused increased tensions throughout the Southwest. In 1875, miners started to invade the Black Hills for gold in South Dakota. Known as the *Paha Sapa* by the Sioux, the land was sacred, and the Sioux were outraged at the desecration. Eventually, armed conflicts between the Sioux, the American miners and the US Army escalated in 1876.

A war for gold had begun prompted by the American Congress withholding food rations for the Native Americans, unless they gave up their land. The inevitable outcome was a loss of many lives and the establishment of the Pine Ridge reservation. Native American tribes in other states would endure similar conflicts. In 1887 the Dawes Act was passed and effected the Native Americans losing control of around one-hundred million acres of land. Later, discovery of valuable materials under what little land the Native Americans had left would become the desire of American corporate imperialism.

Uranium on the Diné Homeland

Native Americans from all nations hold that land is sacred. The Eurocentric notion that land can be split up and owned is against the Native American value system. The earth is regarded as a living entity. Mother Earth is to be cared for and respected. The policies of the United States government were conceived to shove the Native Americans *off to the side* to exploit Mother Earth.

In 1868, the Navajo reservation was established in the corners of Arizona, Colorado, New Mexico and Utah. When the government designated the land to the Navajo (Diné) it was not known that the land had any valuable natural resources. The land was part of the Navajos original settling point after they had migrated from Alaska.

According to Utter, when oil deposits were discovered in northwestern New Mexico in 1921, the Diné had to develop a governing body to make the land use decisions for the Navajo. On July 7, 1923, the first Navajo tribal council was convened in Toadlena, New Mexico, with Chee Dodge as the elected chairman.

In the mid-1950s, the oil industry boomed and brought revenue to the Navajo tribe. The money went to a fund established by the tribal council to benefit all the Diné. Deposits of uranium and coal were also found and exploited. Originally, the council made agreements with the uranium and coal mining companies without consulting the tribal members. The tribal council was also unaware of the extensive damage that would be caused to the land and the community.

The environmental costs of mining are damaging to the environment. In the 1960s, the Navajo Nation worked to expand its resources in coal and uranium. According to Iverson, arrangements were made with the Utah International Mining and Manufacturing Company to mine for coal in 1963; with the Arizona Public Service Company to construct the Four Corners Power Plant also in 1963; and with the Peabody Coal Company to mine coal in 1964. The coal mining operations used large amounts of limited water resources and the power plants caused large amounts of air pollution. Coal waste ponds that are used for mining were contaminated with mercury, lead, thallium and arsenic. The overflow leaked into some areas near the mining sites and where the waste was relocated. Mining companies continue to contaminate the land. This can be illustrated with the example of the Canyon Mine located six miles south of the Grand Canyon. In 2017, contaminated water was literally being sprayed over the land next to the Kaibab National Forest showing the Corporation's lack of respect for the earth as our mother.

Along with the coal and oil industries, uranium mining has also caused extensive damage to the land on the Navajo reservation. The Environmental Protection Agency (EPA) stated that from 1944 through 1986 around four million tons of uranium were mined, leaving behind five hundred and twenty abandoned uranium mines; although, according to Jaffe, the Southwest Research and Information Center estimates that there may be as many as twelve hundred. Wayne Nostri of the EPA acknowledged that some of the sites, "present an imminent and substantial endangerment to human health or the environment.". Uranium mining has left behind mountains of toxic waste called *mine tailings.*

According to the Multicultural Alliance for a Safe Environment, in 1979, the largest release of radioactive waste to ever happen in the US took place when the United Nuclear Corporation uranium mine tailings spill affected communities in the Church Rock area, along the Puerco River in New Mexico and Arizona. Community members have become increasingly more active against mining and in 2005, the Diné Natural Resources Protection Act was established on the Navajo Nation to prevent further irresponsible mining.

Coal and uranium miners were affected by a plague of health problems caused by the mines and have historically suffered from respiratory ailments such as black lung disease. The Native Americans experienced respiratory ailments and other concerns due to poor ventilation, as well. Researchers found that they suffered increased rates of cancer and other chronic disorders, due to the long-term effects caused by toxins. Toxic waste often contaminates water sources as a result of improper disposal. Industries have endangered community members, especially those who are more susceptible to dangerous conditions such as the young and elderly.

The Navajo Nation felt the sharp sting of betrayal from the uranium companies who made it extraordinarily difficult for sick miners to receive compensation for illnesses caused by working in toxic environments. The overall effects of mining have caused a tremendous amount of damage to the Navajo Nation. Although there has been monetary gain, the price of suffering and the loss of lives of those who have absorbed the physical debt from toxifying the environment has not been worth the financial gain.

With coal mining, the Kayenta coal mine made it onto a list of the US top safety violators made by Representative George Miller. The mine problems included unsafe conditions, broken machinery and the lack of first aid equipment. Hazardous conditions led to work related injuries, but the compensation policies created to correct the ailments and injuries were biased.

Power plants surrounded the Great Plains, poisoning the air and toxifying the environment. Strip mines physically destroyed land in the plains and southwest. The Northern Cheyenne in Montana learned the same lessons that the Navajo Nations in Arizona were learning; that strip mines and coal burning power plants had repercussions not worth the damage caused to Mother Earth. The Cheyenne Tribal Council voted to cancel all the coal leases in Montana to stop local strip mining and sued the Department of the Interior in 1973, sparking controversy from the corporations using the land.

Throughout the 1970s, many Tribal Nations had fallen prey to the false promises of the oil, coal and uranium industries. By the 1980s, tribal members of all nations started to become more aware of environmental issues. The Women of All Red Nations (WARN) and the Black Hills Alliance helped educate the people of South Dakota about the damage to their homelands and the possible dumping of toxic waste on the nearby military range.

In 1973, former uranium miner Harry Tome utilized the media to inform the Diné of problems caused by the uranium mines on the Navajo reservation. Activists and grassroots organizations used education through the media as an effective way to combat *environmental racism.* The Environmental Protection Agency reports that at least five-hundred abandoned uranium mines can be connected to water sources and people's homes on the Navajo reservation that have elevated radiation levels. The EPA plans to use money from enforcement agreements and settlements (called superfund settlements) to start the cleanup process. It is shocking that so much time has passed and still little has been done to clean up the mess in 2020.

Environmental Racism in Native America

Environmental racism is a term used to describe the disparity of minority communities that are more likely to be located in areas where corporations and industries that generate pollution, infiltrate. There are many factors that lead to environmental racism and Native American communities are more susceptible to it because they have excessive difficulties with social issues of poverty, unemployment and poor community resources.

Although comprehensive studies have not been undertaken by the government to evaluate the damage done to members of the communities around the mines, many members and researchers believe that the remnants of the mines have poisoned the communities. The EPA has been working at remediating the mines, but for many it has been too little, too late.

CHAPTER 5

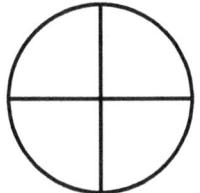

SOUTHWEST TRIBES AND RELIGIOUS OPPRESSION

Missions

As early as the 1500s, Catholic missions found their roots in the conquered blood of defeated Aztecs in Mexico and functioned like small towns. Spanish missions were founded in the southwestern part of North America and in Florida. The purpose of missions was to convert the Indians to Christianity while enslaving them to the mission and forcing them to work for their survival. Indians who resisted the system were whipped, tortured and killed for practicing their traditional beliefs.

Once the tribes were assigned to reservations, the government created a system to *Christianize* the Indians. Congress established resolutions in order to build missions on reservations starting in 1776. The thought – when the Indians adopted Christianity, they would become *good citizens* just like those who oppressed them. The Office of Indian Affairs was governed by Christian religious practitioners who worked primarily at starting missions and boarding schools run by religious groups.

A civilization fund was set aside by Congress in 1819 in order to spread Christian-based missions on reservations. Native American traditional practices were called *heathen* and *pagan,* while medicine men were rebuked by missionaries.

Southwest Tribes and Christianity

American Indians have inhabited the Southwest for over twenty thousand years. The tribes generally developed as agriculture-based villages. The villages along the Rio Grande River in New Mexico were called *pueblos*. The Pueblo Indian's culture and traditional religious practices were intertwined. Native American spiritual beliefs in the Southwest, as well as other places, are based in a spiritual connection to the natural world.

The Pueblo Indians are comprised of twenty-one different tribes located throughout New Mexico and Arizona. They share similar living practices, however, they have different languages or variations of tribal languages and different cultural practices. They were accused of witchcraft and punished for practicing their traditional religious rituals.

In 1539, Fray Marcos de Niza explored the Southwest in search of the fabled cities of silver and gold. He only found the native villages, and later the Spanish would come back seeking a different commodity, the Indian's souls.

In 1598, Don Juan de Oñate started a campaign to forcibly establish Catholic missions throughout the Southwest Pueblo tribes. The priests were accompanied by Spanish soldiers who were armed with metal weapons and armor. The Spanish used military force to take control of the pueblos along the Rio Grande River in central New Mexico. The Spaniards extended their rule westward from the Rio Grande through the Acoma, Zuni and Hopi tribes.

The Spaniards forced the Indians to join the church and work like indentured slaves for the missions under the Spanish flag. They required the Indians to pay tribute to the missions with forced labor, food staples such as corn and grain, and other trade goods. Only to varying degrees of success were the Spaniards able to spread Christianity to tribal groups in the Southwest.

According to Bahti, the Zuni were one of the first groups to resist the Spanish intrusion. Fray Marcos de Niza sent a scout party led by Estevan to the Zuni capital, Hawikuh. The Zuni killed Estevan because he acted in a disrespectful manner and the Spanish later subdued the Zuni with force and built a mission at Hawikuh in 1629. The Zunis live between the Colorado River and the Rio Grande, between the Hopi and the Navajo to the west, and the Acoma to the east. The Zuni had their own distinct language and traditional religious beliefs. Sometimes the Hopi would stay with the Zuni during times of drought, and later the Zuni would shelter some of the Rio Grande pueblo tribes around the time of the Pueblo Revolt in 1680.

Spanish soldiers were sent to the Acoma pueblo off the Rio Grande in order to establish the capital of the mission at the San Juan Pueblo north of the Acoma. The Acoma were able to resist and defeat the Spanish. The Spanish sent more soldiers who killed many of the Indians and destroyed the town. The survivors were made into indentured servants and the surviving males had their right foot chopped off to prevent them from escaping. In 1629, the Franciscans built a mission for the Acoma using forced labor.

The Hopi had a strong Indian religious system when the Spaniards arrived. They initially resisted Spanish rule but were eventually subdued until the Pueblo Revolt as well. The Navajo resisted the Spanish and later raided the missionized pueblos. The Apache groups raided the missionized pueblos and Spanish settlements in Northern Mexico.

The Oke Indians were initially friendly toward the Spaniards, until they started to oppress the Indian's traditional religious practices. In 1675, the Spaniards gathered together forty-seven leaders from the different pueblos and accused them of practicing witchcraft. The pueblo leaders were then whipped. A San Juan medicine man named Popé organized a unified uprising against the Spanish in 1680. Many pueblo tribes revolted against the Spanish by killing the priests, Spanish troops, Spanish settlers and burning down the missions.

Some tribes in the Southwest reacted differently to the Spanish intrusion. The Yaqui and Tohono O'Odham Tribes integrated the Catholic teachings with their own traditional beliefs, mixing the religions. Other tribes, like the Zuni, pretended to accept the Christian beliefs while continuing to practice their traditional Indian rituals in secrecy.

For twelve years, the Indians lived peacefully until Diego de Vargas reconquered most of the New Mexico pueblos. Hundreds of Indians were killed, villages were destroyed and many Indians were sold as slaves. The Native tribes who were reconquered were forced to endure the mission systems until Mexico won the War of Independence from Spain in 1821.

In 1848, the Treaty of Guadalupe Hidalgo ceded control of the Southwest to the US, who flooded the lands with white settlers. Then the Southwest Indians had to face their next group of oppressors.

GREY BEAR STANDS UP

My intent in sharing Native American history is for the reader to understand the context of what it means to be a Native American. This history section starts broadly then leads to the experiences of Native Americans in the Southwest and only a handful of hardships are shared in the book. Also, to completely understand Native Americans one must learn their connection to the earth, which is viewed as a living relation to all humankind.

Environmental racism needs to be actively resisted by Native Americans by educating themselves and others about the potential hazardous threats to them and their communities. Tribal members and councils need to actively promote industries that are beneficial to the environment, and individuals should join groups that encourage education, political growth and activism.

Tribes need to educate themselves about toxic industries. From the 1940s through the 1970s, there was a burst of mining and oil interests found on Native American reservations. These interests were actively sought by corporations such as Union Carbide and others to mine for coal, uranium, and drill for oil. Initially, tribal nations were unaware of the major drawbacks to these operations.

Environmental racism can be prevented by Native Nations. They need to encourage their tribal councils and grassroots organizations to locate and entice beneficial industries to migrate to the reservations. Generally, many Native American reservations have less access to viable industries and job opportunities for tribal members. Unemployment rates on reservations can be as high as ninety percent. As an example, on the Navajo reservation, the rate of members twenty-five years or older who had obtained a high school diploma was forty-one percent in 1990, according to the National Indian Policy Center.

The National Center for Educational Statistics states, "In 2006, twenty-seven percent of American Indian/Alaska Native individuals lived in poverty compared to thirteen percent of the general population. Also, a smaller percentage of American Indian/Alaska Native students (seventy-five percent) reported receiving a high school diploma than White (ninety-one percent)," and had higher unemployment rates than other races. Another factor that plays part in environmental racism is that community members may not be informed of the dangers of industries locating near their communities.

Only through tension caused by controversy can change take place. Members of all nations need to be aware of the costs of any toxic industry encroaching on or near their reservations. Tribal members need to stay informed of how they can participate in protecting their indigenous homeland.

Every man and woman of the Red Nation needs to become involved with environmental racism advocacy by joining or supporting groups that invest in education, political growth and/ or community activism. Native Americans are at the forefront of the battle to protect the Mother Earth from exploitation by greedy corporations. If the Native Americans weren't situated where they are throughout the United States, America would be even more of a toxic wasteland than it is today.

The forests would all be destroyed, the animals all extinct and all the rivers polluted. Native Americans have long been aware of the atrocities committed by the corporate industrial greed system. The rest of America seems to be slowly realizing the true cost and effect of a growing scorched planet. The ocean bled oil from the BP oil spill in 2010, but has that changed anything? The only way that change can ever take place is if someone will begin to act. Native American individuals need to become actively involved in the process to strengthen their communities. Community organizations need to be created that focus on social improvement. The growth of the Red Nation depends on the strength and actions of its members.

Despite all the evidence, corporations and politicians involved in toxic industries like to believe and promote that environmental racism is a myth. They downplay the disadvantages and side effects of hazardous industries being minimal or fabricated. These adversaries may generate their own studies that disprove environmental injuries caused by their industries.

Industry leaders often say that rather than causing harm to the community, toxic industries are beneficial. It is usually easy to see behind the lies and deceit of the corporations when those claims are refuted by their own workers and community members who have been affected. Toxic industries spend a lot of money on lobbying and lawyers to protect their ways. Time is always on their side. It is often the lack of action that benefits the corporations and leads to negative situations for the community.

Environmental racism is a blend of several complex issues that can only be prevented and eradicated by reducing the factors that lead to social injustice. By becoming proactive in preventing environmental racism from future generations, community members can strengthen their tribes. Growth can only be achieved from within. The Sacred Circle of the Red Nation becomes stronger when all tribal nations join together in their actions.

The Indian reservations where Native Americans were relocated has historically been adverse social and physical environments that resulted in higher rates of violence, mortality and social trauma.

According to the Bureau of Justice Statistics in 1999, on a per capita basis, American Indians had a rate of prison incarceration about thirty-eight percent higher than the national rate. Many Native Americans have been the victims of crime or have a family member that has been or is incarcerated. It all started when Christopher Columbus kidnapped, enslaved and incarcerated the first Native Americans. The inter-generational trauma we have experienced has inevitably led many Native Americans to prison, the penological system.

As I have stated previously, the stories intertwine to create a complex blanket. The blanket has covered the eyes of the American people and until they can open their eyes to see the entire process, they will only see something warm and fuzzy; blind to the blood and pain contained therein.

Today, many Indians are still struggling to recover from the trauma that has been afflicted on the Red Nation.

THE AMERICAN PRISON SYSTEM

A TYPICAL DAY IN PRISON LIFE
By Grey Bear

Waking up on a typical weekday in the *iron longhouse,* the first thing you see when you open your eyes, is the institutional ceiling thirty feet above. The panels are like those in school classrooms, white with hundreds of small holes, interspersed with fluorescent lights and vents. I used to wake up, believing I was still at my house in Phoenix, wondering where my girlfriend, son and cat were. Where is my house? I kept waking up to a living nightmare. It's sad, the things you get used to.

Now I wake up automatically between five and six o'clock in the morning. I subconsciously *pick myself up* in the morning when people in the dorm start to get up and use the sinks and showers to get ready for the day. In morning during the winter, the pod is extremely cold. In the summer, it's unbearably hot.

Chow is called from a metal speaker by the door. Everyone starts hustling and bustling. Some who waited until the last-minute, run to the sink for a quick shave (you must shave before you eat, or you will receive a ticket). Most of us are ready and wait by the large steel door for the guard in the control room to let us out. You hear a click and then push past the control room like a stream of orange cattle, rushing to the slaughter. The windows of the control room glare at you in the middle of the four pods while you stand at the next steel door, waiting. The door clicks open to a white hallway that has another steel door at the end of it, where you wait again. The final door opens, the orange cattle run free.

We walk around a paved track, a raceway to the cafeteria. Halfway to the cafeteria, we pass the sweat lodge on the west side of the track, to the east lay the dirt drainage ditch the *Paisas,* the Mexican Nationals use for a soccer field. Paisa is short for paisano. We walk past an old inmate being wheeled on a hospital gurney to medical. He probably came down with the flu that's going around and couldn't get out of bed. That, or a heart attack, that goes around too, for the lifers. Two nurses and four guards accompany him.

The cafeteria is classic prison. A guard checks off your number as you enter, wait in line for food, grab a tray and cup of either burned coffee or a half cup of generic sugar-free Kool-Aid; whichever sounds better. We make our way to the chief table, where all the brothers sit. It is always proper to greet all the brothers before you sit down. Today it's biscuits and gravy. It's actually palatable in the private prison. At the state prison across the street the biscuits and gravy were like *hard tack* (a hard biscuit from the Civil War era) with gravy flavored water. When you're done eating, you place your tray in a window and it disappears. You make your way back to the iron longhouse, it's made of concrete. On the way back we pass the medical line; a line of prisoners waiting at the non-drive thru pharmacy window three times a day for their meds.

We make our way past the white hallway to our steel beds and get ready for the day. Some go back to sleep, some watch TV, some play card and board games all day. A few of us are lucky and have jobs that pay $0.10 to $0.40 an hour during the week.

Every Saturday morning after breakfast, we walk over to the sweat lodge grounds and open the east gate. The grounds are sacred; we walk back to our homeland to be one with Mother Earth. Many moons ago our Spiritual Advisor, Lenny Foster, made these grounds sacred.

Incarcerated Native Americans have to face an uphill battle against oppression when they enter the Arizona Department of Corrections. First, ADOC wants us to prove we are Native American before we can be allowed to practice our religion. Second, Native American beliefs about sacred areas and objects are not recognized by ADOC. Third, when we try to bring these issues up, we face retaliation and we are disregarded. Fourth, some of our religious practices, such as having traditional food at our Pow Wow ceremony, are categorically denied.

CHAPTER 1

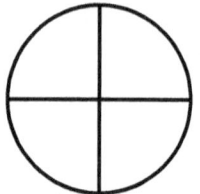

HISTORY OF INCARCERATION

"The prison industry is far more devastating to Native Americans than anything else we encounter in modern times."
Grey Bear

Introduction

The information in this chapter is important for Native American prisoners, their families and for advocates who want to change the prison policy and revolving door of incarceration for Native Americans. Knowing the history of incarceration can be used and applied to the difficulties that Native American prisoners face at this current place and time. According to Echo-Hawk in 1996,

> "As no other segment in American society, Indian prisoners are acutely subject to government restrictions on freedom of worship."

The penological system has historically limited and suppressed religious freedom for Native Americans. The stories have been hidden and lost over time, but with persistence, a picture can be painted in Arizona of the effects of incarceration on Native Americans.

History of Incarceration

Reservations were created to impound the Indians and decimate their numbers. The US military developed stockades to mass incarcerate entire Indian tribes. Also, the jails at that time had no definition of what is considered cruel and unusual treatment.

Many tribes of this Nation have joined under one roof, one that is made of concrete and iron. The prison system is modern slavery and is America's solution to the *Indian Problem.* Virtually every Native American has had a family member in prison or knows someone who has been locked up.

European colonization in the 1600s consisted of Europeans traveling to lands previously unsettled and killing the occupants or enslaving them. The European colonist's concepts of land ownership, time, and crime and punishment were alien to the Native Americans; and the colonist's solution for disputes between the two groups was to establish treaties that took away rights from the Indians and gave land to the colonists.

Every treaty that was ever made was eventually broken! Native Americans were often coerced or unaware of the implication of the treaties that were often made against the wishes of the majority of the tribal members. The treaties were signed under great duress. The one-sided nature of these treaty *dealings* established a precedent for the government's future agreements.

The British took control of Indian Affairs in 1755 and treated the Native Americans as sovereign Nations, because they wanted to retain control of the colonies and used the Indians as political allies. Then, the Revolutionary War that took place from 1775 – 1783 changed the formation of the United States and united the colonies.

In 1778, the newly formed American government had signed its first treaty with the Delaware Indian Tribe. In 1786 the Ordinance for the Regulation of Indian Affairs, a treaty made by Congress to regulate peace between Indians and Non-Indians in the developing territories around the Mississippi River was signed; and in 1787 the Northwest Ordinance, which had a section that stated,

> "...the utmost good faith shall always be observed towards Indians; their land and property shall never be taken from them without their consent..."

was put forth as a good faith agreement by Congress that was never followed. Many acts and orders were written by Congress and the US government in order to take away the Native American's lands and oppress them. Local jails existed in the colonies in the 1700s. In 1789, the United States Constitution was signed; the same year the penitentiary system was established.

The jail system that was established and used by the colonies in America was a brutal system of punishment brought from England that involved stocks, pillories, and the draw and quarter torture. The stock was a wood cross that held a man's arms and head immobile, while the pillory held the feet. Passing colonists would throw rotten food or rocks at the incarcerated. Indian's experienced the same treatment and sometimes their head was shaved to humiliate them; and drawing and quartering was reserved for defiant Indians. The victim was pulled apart alive, then killed and chopped to pieces. The Indian's head was placed on the spiked pole fence colonists used to keep out the Indians. By 1700, William Penn had created the Pennsylvania Criminal Code to be more humane to criminals.

The Philadelphia Society for Alleviating the Miseries of Public Prisons argued for a more humane prison system. Various scholars, criminologists and Christian religious groups began to influence the development of the prison system. For example, *penitence* is the root word for the penitentiary system, having to do with a priest. The system was called the Pennsylvania System and its purpose was reformation. As stated in the Encyclopaedia Britannica, the Auburn system in the nineteenth century modified this system to allow work during the day and forced solitary at night. Silence (no one was allowed to speak) and marching in lockstep (marching in step as the only recreation) were strictly enforced in this system.

Eventually, the penitentiary and British law system joined together in a codependent relationship. No one foresaw how viral and oppressive the *penological system* would become in the United States. The system has grown and changed over time, but the conditions in the prisons remained inhumane with little hope for improvement until 1949 when the Siegal v. Ragen case occurred; an inmate was able to claim protections under the

Eighth Amendment, Fourteenth Amendment and Civil Rights Act.

The US Supreme Court made the decision that would change state courts, giving constitutional Bill of Rights protection to people who had to face the legal system in the 1960s. According to Lowenthal, Chief Justice Earl Warren made sure that the Constitution was the central force guiding the legal system for federal and state offenders. This action lead to a terrible backlash propagated by the media against people's rights.

During the Sixties and Seventies, court cases involving black Muslims helped to shape religious rights in prison. For Native American rights, one of the earliest cases involved a Sioux Indian. According to Echo-Hawk, US ex Rel, Goings v Aaron, 350 F. Supp. 1 (D. Minn. 1972) denied the Sioux Indian the right to wear his hair long for religious purposes.

In the 1970s, states started to impose harsher sentences and limit the power of judges. Ultimate legal power was given into the hands of prosecutors and elected officials who used media propaganda to *con* citizens for votes. Mandatory sentences, aggravating factors and sentencing *enhancements* have resulted in the imprisonment and enslavement of millions of Americans.

Later the Federal Civil Rights Act became the basis of civil rights lawsuits filed by prisoners. In Gittlemacker v. Prasse, (1970), the court determined that the state is obligated to provide inmates the opportunity to practice their religion.

In Cruz v. Beto in 1972, the court decided that it would be discriminatory for a Buddhist prisoner to be denied a reasonable opportunity to pursue his faith as compared to other more conventional practices of other inmates.

In 1971, the Native American Rights Fund (NARF) was established as a Native American advocacy organization; and in 1972, NARF started the Indian Corrections Project, which operated until 1981. NARF attorneys testified before the Senate in 1978 in support of the American Indian Religious Freedom Act (AMRFA). Litigation for Native American prisoners from

1970 to 1987 was effective in protecting Native American rights, as long as the Native American prisoners were willing to endure the retaliation involved from prison officials. According to Walter Echo-Hawk,

> "Since 1970, this continuing human rights problem has been the subject of over fifty lawsuits to protect the First Amendment rights of Native American prisoners."

Native American prisoners won the rights for access to medicine men, sweat lodges, pipe ceremonies, sacred objects, traditional hair length, head bands and religious medallions starting in the 1970s and their rights continues today.

At the beginning of 1980, prisons held five hundred thousand souls and as of 2018, According to the BJS report American Indians and Crime (1999),

> "On a per capita basis, American Indians had a rate of prison incarceration about 38% higher than the national rate."

The government changed its tactics in the *war on poverty* to a *war against the impoverished;* shipping minorities to prisons.

Also, the media fueled by reports from law enforcement and prosecutors, fabricated an imaginary epidemic of drug and crime waves caused supposedly by crack cocaine. The low price and easy accessibility of crack was supposedly the cause of economic blight in the American ghettoes. Legislators throughout the US reacted to combat the imaginary drug epidemic and federal acts against crack possession, creating a one hundred to one sentencing disparity between powder cocaine and crack with the Anti-Drug Abuse Act in 1986. Later the Fair Sentencing Act made it an eighteen to one disparity.

The result was that law enforcement targeted the poor neighborhoods where offenders were least likely to have the ability to retain a lawyer. The conditions in the poor neighborhoods have remained the same and wave after wave of minorities have filled the prison system, not due to an increase in crime, but a change in the definition of it. Crime rates dropped in the 1990s, but the numbers of incarcerated people kept rising.

For various reasons, less than half of crimes that occur are reported. Criminology statistics on law enforcement are mired with confounding variables. At the base level, when an arrest is made, officers in different areas and situations report crimes at their discretion. *According to the US Department of Education in 2016, more money is spent incarcerating Americans than educating them.* According to Prison Policy Initiative, in 2018, approximately 2.3 million people were incarcerated in the United States, leading to the thought that the primary purpose of incarceration is profit; using the façade of *public safety*. Politicians, law enforcement and the American media have created an ideology that differs from the rest of the world.

CHAPTER 2

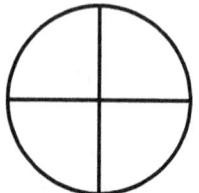

ARIZONA DEPARTMENT OF CORRECTIONS PROTOCOL AND POLICY

Introduction

Many lawsuits have been filed by Native American prisoners to protect their free exercise of religion. These claims are not always guaranteed to win, as the outcome depends largely on prior case law. The penological system has failed Native America, as prisons are institutions of Christian propaganda that have actively repressed the Natives spiritual practices.

Native American spirituality benefits the Indian prisoners, their family and Native society, yet prison officials actively undermine and try to deter Native Americans from seeking traditional Native American spiritual practices.

The Navajo Nation, located in Northeastern Arizona, New Mexico and Utah is the largest tribe in the US and the reservation covers over eighteen thousand square miles. The Navajo tribe sponsors the Navajo Nation Corrections Project under the direction of Len Foster. Len and Walter Echo-Hawk have been on the outside, yelling to the bureaucrats that the forest of religious rights was on fire. They were trying to obtain a directive from then Attorney General Janet Reno to increase Federal protection for the free exercise of religion by Native American prisoners.

Very few writings concerning Native American prisoners exist. Rose Ann Kisto was contracted by the Arizona Department of Corrections (ADOC) in 1994 to write a manual about Native American beliefs. Rose Ann consulted Len Foster as she wrote the manual. Some sections of the manual regarding Native American religious practices were similar to the ADOC prison policy at the time.

The *Study of Native American Prisoners Issues* was written by Walter Echo-Hawk in 1996 for the National Indian Policy Center; while the articles: *Sweat Lodges in American Prisons* written by Jacob Stroub in 2005, *Incarceration of Native Americans and Private Prisons* by Frank Smith and *Walking the Red Road in the Iron House* by Joel West Williams both written in 2014; can be found in various journals. These publications paint a picture of the issues that Native Americans face in prison, while these chapters focus on issues faced in a specific Arizona prison.

CHAPTER 3

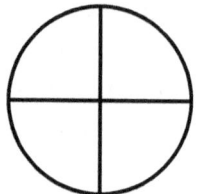

RELIGIOUS INTOLERANCE AMONG NATIVE AMERICAN PRISONERS

Native American Brotherhood

In 1979 a group of Native American inmates banded together to form a religious group and called themselves the Native American Brotherhood (NAB). The group organized itself as a club, per ADOC policy, and were active in obtaining policy provisions for a sweat lodge, Pow Wow, pipe ceremony and talking circle from 1979 to 1996. The Brotherhood had a group account and was actively involved in fundraising for the Pow Wows, buying wood and rocks for sweat ceremonies, and gaining access to religious items and instruments as they were needed. However, the rights that the NAB once fought for in the Arizona correctional system, have since been *unwritten.*

More than thirty years have passed since the policy that contained provisions for Native religion was created. But no sweat lodge provision existed in ADOCs policy as it related to obtaining firewood, until Grey Bear's court case. The Native Americans experienced restrictions that have substantially burdened their religion and right to practice their faith. Unfortunately, Native Americans have little clue of how they arrived at the place they are in today regarding their religious rights in prison.

Many sweat lodges were established in the period in which

the Native American Brotherhood period existed at the ADOC (~1980s). From 1992 – 1996 Native American advocates and organizations spoke out against religious discrimination that Native American prisoners experienced. In 1992 Native Americans testified before the 102nd Congress about oppressive practices of prison officials toward Native American spiritual practitioners.

In the ADOC *Native American Religious Services Program Manual,* policy was included in the manual and it contained requirements for the sweat lodge, talking circle, pipe ceremony and Pow Wow ceremony. Most of the requirements have disappeared over time, although the wording hasn't changed for those few requisites that still exist.

In October 1992, the Native American Rights Fund sent a survey to all US state and federal correctional facilities to assess their Native American religious policies. An attachment to religious policy called DMP207.0-A was referred to in Kisto's *Native American Religious Services Program Manual* revision in July 1994. DMP 207.0-A *Religious Exemptions to Policy – Native American* states the following in regard to religious items:

> "Native American – medicine bag and its contents. Note: This is a holy object, if an inspection of the contents is needed, the Chaplain should be contacted to make the inspection, headbands – leather, beaded, or cloth. Up to four headbands of black, red, yellow, green, blue or white solid or patterns. Headbands may be worn at any time; one shell for smudging, e.g. burning sage, etc. or for ceremonial cleansing of self or surroundings. One ounce each of sage – one ounce; sweet grass – one ounce and tobacco – four ounces; sacred stones, up to seven marble sized, ½" in diameter; Eagle feather, corn husks, corn pollen, other feathers (number to be determined); and any other traditional items and materials sanctioned by the Native American community and approved by the director – security personnel may not touch, animal parts e.g., eagle bone whistle, two small bones, bone necklace strung on a string, tooth, or skin. Note: Often

these items are decorated with beadwork or leather. With the Chaplain's consent and proper security checks, these items are considered religious, not hobbies, and may be found in a Native American's property."

These provisions for religious property and ceremonies were the best that would be allowed in the prison system. Over time the Native American inmates lost nearly all these provisions.

Religious Intolerance, Injustice and ADOC Policy

The ADOC treated their Native American religious policy just like the United States has treated all its own treaties with Native Americans. By breaking all their own rules and rewriting the policy, the Arizona correctional system removed the rights of the Native Americans. When looking at older policies regarding the religious practice of Native Americans, one can see the removal of several practices. For example, a spiritual feast was allowed as part of the Pow Wow ceremony in prior policy. At the time of this writing no food is mentioned in the policy and when Native American prisoners asked for food during the ceremony, it was denied.

It is an unfortunate irony that Native American prisoners are spiritually oppressed in North American prisons. Christianity is repressed in other countries, yet in America it is pushed on inmates. Constitutional protections are ignored within the concrete barriers of the prison microcosm. Prisons openly violate the First Amendment Freedom of Exercise clause, the Establishment Clause and the Fourteenth Amendment right to equal protection.

Christian prisoners have many opportunities to gather together for their ceremonies; in most cases every day of the week, while Native American and other non-Christian groups are limited to only one turnout per week. If the Christians want to have a Bible study on their own time they are often encouraged and even given a space in the recreation room or another area, to conduct their study. When Native Americans try to gather for a talking circle they are told to break it up. On rare occasions when the Native Americans gained approval to conduct a smudge from the chaplain's office, the security officers still broke it up. ADOC policy 904/4.1.8.1-2 (2016) states,

> 4.1.8.1.1
> Smudging (smoldering herbs) by followers of religious traditions that smudge is permitted, unless specifically restricted by the custody level and security of the unit.
>
> 4.1.8.1.2
> Locations and times of this activity shall be determined by Senior Chaplains and Deputy Wardens.

Native American prisoners in Arizona were locked out of their sacred area (sweat lodge grounds). They were only allowed to use their religious area, if there was wood available for a sweat ceremony and the sweat was taking place. If no wood was available, the chaplains wanted the Native Americans to use the multi-denominational chapel that was filled with Christian Bibles, books and pamphlets. It is believed by the Native inmates that these actions are an attempt to *Christianize the Indians.*

Native American inmates were free to use the sweat lodge ground during their recreation time for private prayer, gathering together and to assist the sweat lodge porter in maintaining the Native American's sacred religious area, but ended when the Native Americans at the prison decided to stand up for their rights.

Arizona Department of Corrections (ADOC) religious policy 900/904, 1.5.3. from 1996 states:

> "Talking circles are religious ceremonies generally conducted on a weekly basis. The frequency and details shall be arranged through the Chaplain, in consultation with the Warden, Deputy Warden, or Chief of Security."

In 2008, Native American prisoners in Arizona were subject to a rule that was not expressly written in policy. Administration wanted Native American prisoners to use the chapel for their religious practice, but the Native inmates wanted to use their sweat lodge area for talking circles when a sweat ceremony wasn't taking place. This rule was originally posted as a memo, but was never added to religious policy. It was one of the *hidden* rules that existed in ADOCs religious policy.

The ADOC administration's desire to control the Native Americans and their religious rights is found in their unwritten policies. The overall policy was written in a way that covers the actions of the administrators and officers. When the administration acted outside of policy, as they often did, they would not admit it and cite *security* or monetary reasons to explain the administration's actions.

For example: originally when the fence was put up around the sweat lodge, the brothers asked for gates at the openings to protect the area. The officers refused, citing security reasons. Years later, in June 2009, gates and locks were placed on the lodge fence after officers and the Chaplain desecrated it in May 2009, citing security reasons. The administration changed the rules as they needed, with complete disregard for the Native American's constitutional rights regarding freedom to practice religion.

Another instance occurred when Grey Bear wrote a letter to the Senior Chaplain, who was the Administrator of Pastoral Activities for ADOC,

> "There is a rule, not stated in policy that prohibits the Native American sweat lodge group from using their religious area, the sweat lodge grounds, if there is no wood for a sweat ceremony. If there is no wood during the turnout, we are told that we must use the Christian Chapel for a talking circle. We would rather not do that because we need to smudge outside and we pray to Father Sky and Mother Earth outside with our song. There is no rational reason why we can't be allowed to pray in our sweat lodge area. Why are we locked out of our sacred grounds?"

The Senior Chaplain replied,

> "The sweat lodge area does not belong to the *Native American sweat lodge group* as you contend. It exists

for the sole purpose of housing the sweat lodge and therefore, should only be accessed for sweat ceremonies. There is no *Christian chapel* and religious groups utilize multi-purpose rooms for services/ceremonies. Smoke generating ceremonies must be held outdoors in an area designated by prison administration (not the sweat lodge)."

This was one of many times that Grey Bear stood up for his people. The interaction between him and the Chaplain ended up with the Native brothers boycotting all religious ceremonies. A few months later the Native inmates gathered outdoors to participate in their weekly talking circle regardless of the Chaplain's request to gather indoors. This issue was won in Grey Bear's court case and led to the Pastoral Activities Administrator stating that all smoke generating ceremonies needed to be held outdoors.

Spiritual Advisors and Chaplains

At each prison within the Arizona Department of Corrections, there is generally only one chaplain who is present during the week. This chaplain coordinates a variety of religious activities for all the inmates at the prison, who are grouped into many different religions. Other chaplains are allowed in the prison to conduct sessions or turnouts in order for the inmates to worship.

Christians have a pastor, Catholics have a priest, Jewish groups have a rabbi, and Native American groups have spiritual advisors. A spiritual advisor is a shaman, pipe holder, or other practitioner who can perform Native American ceremonies for the Native American inmates. There are few spiritual advisors available for Native American inmates and it is rare for one to visit. When no advisor is available, the prison chaplain will still allow prisoners to gather for their religious practice.

It's not unusual for a prison chaplain to stay a year or two then move on to another job, and the prison where Grey Bear was incarcerated was no different. The prison had gone through several chaplains and each one brought a new set of rules and restrictions. For the Christian groups, a new chaplain often brings new opportunities to practice their faith, while the non-Christian groups experience new restrictions that oppress their religious exercise. In one instance, the chaplain followed the rule book and did everything according to policy. The problem was that the ADOC religious policy lacked the proper provisions to protect Native American religious exercise.

Without Native American spiritual advisors visiting the prisoners on a regular basis, there will be conflict. Advisors can explain to prison administrators the beliefs of the Native American prisoners and give guidance on how to conduct proper searches of sacred Native American objects and the sweat lodge. Spiritual Advisors can be a bridge of communication that will prevent conflict. Unfortunately, there are few, if any, advisors available in Arizona.

Searches

The central problem to conflicts in Arizona prisons was a lack of protection for Native American religious items and the sweat lodge. Policy might state that *appropriate* respect shall be given to *sacred* items, but without any references for officers to understand the Native American beliefs, they are clueless as to how to give proper respect to sacred objects.

When an officer conducts a search of an inmate's area in an ADOC prison, the inmate must be present to witness the search. In most cases, this is protocol. When the officer searches the Native American inmate's religious box he may ask the inmate to move the items around in order to view its total contents. If something is wrong with the box, the officer can confiscate the box and have is searched by the chaplain.

Technically, there are no protocols listed in ADOC policy on how a religious box is to be searched, so officers can easily desecrate sacred items. An untrained officer will reach into the box and grab the sacred items, often infuriating the Native American. The only remedy for a desecrated item or box is to burn it in the fire pit.

Quarterly searches are conducted in prison. This search is different from a regular search, in that inmates aren't allowed to be present during the quarterly search. The entire dorm is taken to a room where each inmate is strip searched and then waits in another area, usually the basketball court, until the search is over. In order to conduct the searches of the entire inmate population, non-security officers also assist in the procedure.

These officers are often unfamiliar with Native Americans beliefs and routinely desecrate Native American religious items. Grey Bear made the mistake of leaving his medicine bag in his religious box during a quarterly search. When the search was over, he returned to his bunk and found that his medicine bag had been emptied out, refilled and left untied. This was a serious desecration of religious property and he felt he had to burn the bag according to tradition, and buy a new medicine bag.

The elder Natives knew the procedure for searches, as most of the Native American's beliefs are passed from person to person by oral tradition. Grey Bear learned that the search guidelines for the sweat lodge had been written down by the Native American Brotherhood decades earlier when he received a copy of it from an elder brother.

Rules of Darkness

When Grey Bear was asked why he got involved in the religious rights of the Native American in prison, he answered that he believed that their rights were flawed and unconstitutional. He knew there were ways around the correctional system and he believed in the right to practice their religion, like they have for thousands of years.

From Grey Bear's perspective, the correctional institution has unwritten policies known as the *Rules of the Darkness*. There are others, but these three unspoken administration rules keep most inmates silent. They include:

- Never admit to any wrong-doing. Everything is *justified* by policy.

- If the inmate uses policy against the officer, the policy must be denied, rewritten or removed; the officer is always right.

- If the inmate complains on paper (grievance) he must be harassed, sent to *the hole* (administrative segregation) or *shipped off* to another next unit.

There are unwritten rules for the inmates as well. They include:

- Never put your name on paper.
- Never stir things up.
- Accept things as they are.

Conflict with regards to Native American rights is caused from two separate goals from two separate sources. The goal of the penological institution is *control* under the guise of security or the prison's best interest. The goal of the Native American is to practice an existing way of life that goes beyond the definition of religion.

Grey Bear wrote a manifest to the prison administrators in response to the religious conflict he and the other inmates experienced; it will be explained later in the book. Much of what was originally written was repetitive because what started as a proposal to the administration grew each time the officials added more adverse reactions to the initial conflict. Within six months of sending the manifest virtually all the issues with Native American rights were addressed and oppressed.

It started with one letter from Irene Herder, Legislative Associate, regarding an update on the National Native American Prisoners Rights Advocacy Coalition (NNAPRAC) meetings in Denver, Colorado. Dated December 16, 1996, it was addressed to Albert Hale, President of the Navajo Nation, Washington Office. One of the Native American brothers gave Grey Bear a copy of the letter, which had been passed around among the inmates for over ten years. Like an ancient weapon, Grey Bear realized it could be formed into a manifest for the Native brother's right to worship their Creator. Words can become great power if placed in the right hands and acted upon.

Quiet Oppression

Religious policy for the Native Americans was its strongest in 1994, but waves of oppression led to inequality. With ADOCs anti-Indian religious policy, the Native brothers were in a bad situation. The Native Americans didn't realize it because they had not been *watching over* their religious policy. Someone *at the top* in the correctional agency had been discreetly erasing the Native American rights out of its policy. Some of the brothers who had been in prison a long time gave Grey Bear copies of old paperwork and policies that dealt with the Native American religious group.

The problems the Native inmates were experiencing were due to well-crafted loopholes placed in policy. Every part of Native American religion was restricted in some way, either by misleading policy that gave the appearance of protecting Native rights but did not; or the lack of policy. The loopholes were very well written and in May 2009, an incident caused a ripple effect in one of Arizona's newest prisons that would change everything and prompted Grey Bear to stand up for his people by filing a Federal lawsuit. By the end of 2010, ADOC stopped supplying the Native Americans wood for the only religious right they had left, the sweat lodge ceremony.

Grey Bear realized that there was an entire prison system full of religious intolerance directed at Native American prisoners. Native Americans had been bullied into silence so many times that there was no standard of religious equality anymore. The only time prison officials would sit at the table with the brothers was when they took away a right.

CHAPTER 4

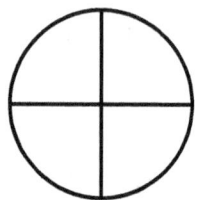

ENROLLMENT

We Have to Prove We Are Native by Spotted Owl

It all started when I was arrested. The detective asked me my race and I told him, "Eskimo!"

"Ah," he said, "So do you want to be put as white or Indian?"

I looked at him and said, "They are Native Americans!" He looked at me again and said, "So what is it going to be?"

I was thinking to myself, "Where did he go to school?" He didn't know who an Eskimo or a Native American is and he's a detective. I told him, "An Indian!" Apparently, he thought Alaska was a European Country.

It took the court system three months to sentence me, and another two weeks to send me to the intake facility. The same thing happened again. A white man asked my race and I told him "Eskimo!" At the time, I thought he wrote Native American on my AIMS (ADOCs computer record system) file. Six days later I was sent to the yard.

I arrived at the prison and was placed in a cell with a white guy. Another white guy came over and asked me if I was Native American or white. I told him, "I'm a Native American." He introduced me to another Native American in the bunk bed setup, and we went to talk to the CPO III about the reason I was bunked with a white guy. She looked on my AIMS file and mentioned that I was categorized as Caucasian (white). I told her the white man at the intake facility couldn't tell that I'm Native American; even though I told him that I was Eskimo! My CPO III told me that I would have to provide documentation, like my Certificate of Indian Blood (CIB) to prove that I'm Native American.

The next day I moved to the bunk with the other Native American. He shared with me everything about living in the same area with the Native Americans – keeping our area nice and neat, bed made, face washed, teeth brushed, hair combed, clean clothes, and so on. He showed me where they sat to eat breakfast, lunch and dinner, and where the *sweats* took place every Saturday. He also introduced me to the other Native Americans on the yard. He explained to the others what happened, and they said it was okay, but obtain the paperwork ASAP. This took place at the beginning of November.

My *cellie* knew another Native American who has *his woman* in Alaska. I contacted her to obtain the address of the enrollment department of the Bureau of Indian Affairs. In the letter I requested my CIB, in order to change my race on my AIMS file.

A couple months passed and I asked the Native brother if he found the address, as I still hadn't received an answer. I asked my CPO III and some of my teachers in *Programs* if they could help. I wrote to my family and called my girlfriend and asked for their assistance in obtaining the address for me; but nothing.

By now I was upset with the whole situation and was close to giving up. Then, one day I was at the library and saw a book in the Native American section called *American Indians: Answers to Today's Questions* by Jack Utter. I checked out the book, started reading it and found a lot of information, including the addresses I needed. I also found the office addresses for the Bureau of Indian Affairs and the Alaska Federation of Natives. Surprisingly, I even found my great-great grandpa's name in the book. It was really cool to see his name in print.

I wrote to the Bureau of Indian Affairs in Juneau, Alaska to get my Certificate of Indian Blood. I gave them my tribe and my father's name and asked for my CIB because I was already registered. I waited. About a month later I received a letter from the BIA and when I opened it, an application form to be enrolled with the BIA was enclosed. It didn't do me any good because I was already enrolled.

Next, I wrote to the Alaska Federation of Natives in Anchorage, Alaska. I believe they forwarded my letter to the enrollment department because about a month later, I received my CIB. From start to finish, it took five to six months to get my CIB.

Now I had my CIB but needed to get my race changed on my AIMS file. That took some work. First, I met with the acting Chaplain, who also was the CPO III for my dorm. He took my CIB so he could give it to Central Office and have my file changed. Told to check back with him in a week, I did, only to be told by him that it was a forgery because it was printed from a computer. I said, "What are you, crazy?" He asked if I had family in Anchorage and I told him no! The Chaplain said he would take the CIB to another unit to determine if it was real. He told me to return in two days and he would have an answer.

Two days later, I returned to see the acting Chaplain. When I asked what they said, he told me he didn't go. I was so mad. I told him to return the CIB and I would take care of everything on my own! He handed me the CIB and as I left, he asked me to have a copy made at the library so he could take it to the other unit. I told him, "No! I'll take care of it myself!" I walked out of the chapel.

The next day, I sent a kite to the Deputy Warden explaining what happened, and an old *cellie* also talked to the Deputy Warden about the situation on my behalf. A few days later I met with the Deputy Warden and explained the situation in detail. I asked him if he would review my paperwork and he agreed. I went to my dorm, retrieved the paperwork, returned and handed him the application from the BIA. I explained that I was already enrolled with the BIA and showed him my CIB. Alaska processes the paperwork differently than the BIA and tribal offices in the lower forty-eight states.

A week later, the Deputy Warden sent me a kite stating the

matter was addressed and when I checked with my CPO III, my AIMS file was updated. It was a battle because friends and family didn't want to help. The library book provided all the information I needed to obtain my CIB. It took about six months, but worth the wait.

My Personal Enrollment Experience with The Arizona Prison System By Grey Bear

Becoming a practitioner of Native American religion can be an ordeal in some state prisons. In Arizona, I had problems gaining sweat lodge membership and know many other Natives who had the same problem. We had many non-official members who weren't allowed on the participation list, but still joined us every Saturday for our service. When an incoming inmate is initially classified by race, he is subject to the discretion and discrimination of the prison officer who happens to be on duty at the time of *intake*. For some reason, those officers don't like to classify Indians as Indians. Many of us have mixed blood and are confused as to why a race has to be *chosen*. I am of the human race.

Native Americans are often classified incorrectly, and prison officials can make it difficult to prove membership. "That doesn't sound like an Indian name," the officer told me as I was being processed upon entry into prison. I tried to explain to the officer that when the Native Americans in my tribe (Mohave) were placed on reservations, some were given the last name of the soldiers classifying them.

Obtaining CIB paperwork from inside the prison can be difficult and sometimes impossible. The tribe of which I am a member, never sent my proof of tribal citizenship even though I wrote them twice.

Also, officers make you chose a religious preference. No Native American living in America considers their religion to be *Native American*. Being a part of the Great Hoop, being a follower of the Red Road or Corn Pollen Road is not an option for us; Native American spirituality goes deeper than any bloodline or label. Everybody and everything are related, no matter how people try to separate themselves from one another. Many Native Americans consider themselves to be Christian, attending Christian services and bible studies, while also joining talking circles and sweat ceremonies. This is perfectly normal and acceptable.

Unfortunately, the Christian chaplains try to prevent inmates from practicing two religions. On one occasion, the Chaplain posted warning notices stating that any person attending a *turnout* (religious service) whose name was not on the list would be *subject to disciplinary action.* This was considered by the Natives, an overt threat, not that anybody paid attention to the notice.

Not all tribes are recognized by the United States and others have been *terminated.* Some Indians have been adopted or placed in foster care, so obtaining paperwork can be difficult. Canadian, Hawaiian, Alaskan and Mexican (like the Yaqui) tribes are often misclassified.

In 1993, the Arizona Department of Corrections required that the Native American Religious Service Program contractor approve the sweat lodge group membership. Originally there were four ways to obtain approval from the contractor or spiritual advisor. The first and easiest approval was for the Native American who already had verification from prior membership or had their paperwork from their tribe.

The second, the contractor would temporarily allow the membership while the contractor would contact the tribe to verify tribal enrollment. The third approval occurred when a Native American had not yet enrolled with his tribe. They were allowed a conditional membership until he was able to enroll which could take several months, or they could obtain sponsored membership. The fourth way for a Native American to obtain approval was for the contractor to sponsor membership to a non-Indian or for an Indian who was unable gain enrollment information. At any given Native American service there are several *unofficial* members because of a policy that is discriminative against Native Americans. Native Americans have never and will never use ethnicity as a sole factor for sweat lodge turnout membership.

Today, the ADOC Native American religious policy appears to allow the Spiritual Advisor to be responsible for Native American religious membership; however, this is never the case. Instead, chaplains in Arizona's prisons often issue blanket denials of membership. As a volunteer teacher in prison, I once had a Navajo student who looked, spoke and had the obvious last name of a Navajo. When the Chaplain denied his membership my Diné brother was insulted and refused to re-apply for membership. Unfortunately, this attitude and action is very common.

CHAPTER 5

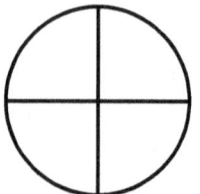

ARIZONA DEPARTMENT OF CORRECTION'S RESPONSE TO SWEAT LODGE DESECRATION

Eagle came back with a big stack of kites. Grey Bear drafted a general informal grievance for the brothers to copy. He told the brothers that problem number four was optional, which said that a woman was allowed into the sweat lodge.

In retrospect Grey Deer, a Hopi and the number two person in the religious leadership was right; he already knew how the prison officials would twist that statement, and Grey Bear made the mistake of being too vague. But in his mind, he knew that unless officers would learn what the Native American's beliefs were regarding sacred objects, officers would keep on desecrating them. The draft of the informal grievance stated:

> "Informal grievance – we would like to receive a group grievance form on this issue. Our Native American sweat lodge has holes in it and artwork was smashed up. We were informed as a group by the Pastor what happened, we feel that our area was desecrated. There are several issues we would like to address with the grievance system.
>
> > 1. Religious sensitivity issues.
> > 2. Defacing sweat lodge without justification.
> > 3. Defacing sand sculpture artwork.

4. Female allowed into sweat lodge.
5. Rocks touched by officers.

The sweat lodge sanctity has been breached. We as a group would like:

1. Re-blessing set for the sweat lodge.
2. Officers informed of religious sensitivity.
3. Policy written regarding how to be respectful when entering sacred grounds.
4. Guarantee that changes have been made to prevent further issues.
5. Official written statement of apology from staff."

Prayers for Relief

The first concern involved the officers' complete lack of training for religious sensitivity. Grey Deer shared with the sweat lodge participants that in the days of the NAB, the prisons held a weekly class for officers that addressed Native American beliefs. The *Native American Services Program Manual* should have been made available to officers, but Arizona prison officials acted as if the manual didn't exist. Whenever the Native inmates gave information to the prison officials regarding their religion, the information would disappear; even though a manual was available.

The Native Americans felt as if the prison officials in Arizona refused to acknowledge their beliefs. Since the sweat lodge was unusable, they asked for a new sweat lodge and for it to be re-blessed. This was the first prayer for relief.

The second concern dealt with the officers defacing and desecrating the sweat lodge without justification. The officers claimed they were justified in their actions but refused to provide any evidence. The Native brothers asked for evidence of the alleged wires or nails, but the officers failed to produce it. The Native brothers asked to review the surveillance video of the sweat lodge's search, but the officers claimed, "We don't save that." This was hard for the Native Americans to believe, as an investigation that leads to any type of drug, gambling or fight activity, surveillance video is accessible to the officers for review weeks after the event occurred.

The brothers were told by one security officer, that the videos were saved forever and probably archived. When the *lines were drawn in the sand,* the Chaplain and prison officials joined together to retaliate against the Native Americans by throwing the water drum in the trash and building gates around the sweat lodge, while security remained neutral. Photographs of the damage to the sweat lodge were taken, but when the inmates asked for copies, the officers claimed that they were erased. The Native American inmates asked the Chaplain and prison administrators that the officers be informed of religious sensitivity; the second prayer for relief.

The third issue dealt with the defacement of the symbols the Native brothers had carved into the sand. Eagle, their pipe holder, would carve Native American symbols and pictures into the area around the lodge in order to keep people from trampling the sacred land. This land was outside the sweat lodge fence and was designated sacred.

On the day of the sweat lodge desecration, Eagle had drawn a turtle symbol split into four quarters in the sand. Within the four quarters was a different aspect of Native American culture.

In one quarter was a medicine wheel that symbolized healing; in another quarter was a sun that represented the children; another had the symbol of a woman that represented the woman spirit, and in the last quarter was a feather that represented the warrior spirit.

Sometime either before or after the sweat lodge search, an officer or officers wiped the symbols out with their boots. Their behavior showed the mindset of the officers on that day. The officers never admitted to wiping out the symbols or explained why the action was taken. If they had asked the sweat lodge members to remove the symbols, it would have been done in a manner that was respectful to the Creator and Mother Earth. The officers were unaware of the symbolism and how to respect the sand drawings. The third prayer for relief— policy to be written explaining how to be respectful when entering Native American sacred grounds.

The fourth concern dealt with allowing a female into the sweat lodge. A tremendous amount of misunderstanding would be generated from this statement. It is OK for a female to be in the sacred area, as long as the moontime tradition was respected, as this tradition has been handed down from their ancestors. Prison officials would later accuse the Native Americans of being discriminatory against women. The fourth prayer for relief— a change was needed to the existing religious policy in order to prevent further moontime issues.

The fifth issue that concerned the Native inmates dealt with the rocks that were used for the sweat lodge ceremony; they had been touched by the officers. The rocks are *their ancestors* and are very sacred. The Native Americans viewed the rocks as sacred ancestors and by touching them, the officers desecrated them. When one knows and understands what the sacred rocks represent, and respects them as an elder, only then may the rocks be handled; as it will be done in a respectful manner. The officers disrespected the rocks and the sweat lodge that day. The final prayer— to receive an official written statement of apology from the ADOC staff.

Eagle and Grey Deer informed the circle that once the paperwork process started, they needed to complete its course, no matter what happened. They said that once the paperwork was submitted to ADOC, the sweat lodge brothers would face a lot of retaliation from the prison system. It turned out, those words would be an understatement.

The *brothers* sat around the sweat lodge area and copied the grievance template that Grey Bear had written. Some of the brothers opted out of writing paperwork for fear of retaliation that they were sure would follow. Some brothers asked Grey Bear to write their informal grievances and they would sign it.

When the brothers completed writing their grievances, Eagle finished the ceremony with a closing prayer. The Native inmates prayed that the prison officials would wake up to see the error of their ways. As a group, they hung around the sweat lodge and played the kettle drum, a sacred symbol of the Native American Church. They sang for their ancestors and all creation, for Mother Earth and Father Sky and for their people, the Red Nation.

As Grey Bear walked into his dorm, he saw some of the other brothers standing in the counselor's office; they were turning in their informal grievances. There was no turning back.

CHAPTER 6

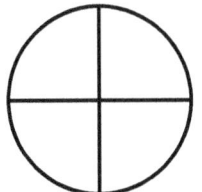

KITES, INMATE LETTERS & GRIEVANCES

Inmate Letter (IML)

An inmate letter form (IML) is provided to inmates by the Arizona Department of Corrections (ADOC) in order for them to communicate with officers and officials of ADOC. These IML forms are sent to the chaplain to request religious items and activities, to the counselor for various services, and to prison administrators for requests and complaints.

Some officials won't answer a kite, letter, grievance or proposal on paper; rather, they call you into their office and deal with issues verbally. On one occasion, Grey Bear wrote an IML about firewood that was needed for the sweat ceremony. While Grey Bear who worked during the day as a Mandatory Literacy and GED teacher's aide was in the classroom, a correctional program supervisor entered. Grey Bear left the classroom and followed the CPS to his office to discuss the issues Grey Bear had presented about the sweat lodge policy as it related to firewood.

There wasn't much to discuss from Grey Bear's viewpoint, as arrangements had already been made for a sponsor to bring wood into the prison and for it to be stored in the designated area. Unfortunately, the arrangement was only a one-time deal, and a system had not been set in place for a steady source of wood.

Grey Bear had a meeting with the Warden of the prison, the Chaplain, and a supervisor of the correctional officer. During the meeting, no direct answers were given to Grey Bear regarding the IML he submitted about a proposal he wrote regarding wood for the sweat lodge. The meeting did clarify that ADOC policy would only allow a sponsored group to bring wood inside the prison and this process wasn't working well. For the next seven weeks, the brothers went without a sweat. The only option left was to take the proposal about the sweat lodge and wood to the Warden himself.

When Grey Bear gathered with the older brothers at the circle that weekend, he learned some information that explained why things were happening. Back in the day, when the Native American Brotherhood was a club, the group did have a group account in order to fundraise. Fundraising is common in prison, as it allows groups to raise money for various projects, and in this case, to buy wood for the sweat. But, according to Kisto, ADOC refused to give official recognition to the NAB (Native American Brotherhood) and NAS (Native American Sisterhood) as an actual faith group, so many NAB and NAS groups were forced to organize under the Programs Department as a club. This *reorganization* was done in order to receive assistance from the department in fundraising for Pow Wows, gathering and distributing firewood and rocks for the sweat lodge, and being released from work and school in order to attend religious services.

Different religious groups had registered as clubs as well. But somewhere along the line, the groups were no longer recognized as clubs and ADOC put a stop to all the fundraising and fund gathering. Technically, there are no restrictions against fundraising and group accounts, but if there are no provisions to allow these things in policy, then the lack of policy is the restriction.

Even if the brothers gained approval for *anything* they requested from the Warden, the fix would only be temporary and would eventually be overturned. This action was not uncommon; as in the case of Grey Bear's beadwork kit that was approved one month and the next month the rules changed. It was now considered contraband and taken from him.

Knowing the possible action by ADOC, Grey Bear did not take the proposal to the Warden. Instead, he had another plan in mind as a solution that was only available from top level executives.

In February 2010, Grey Bear wrote an inmate letter to the Chaplain stating,

> "The sweat lodge members would like to make a request. Our group has expressed the desire to have a talking circle during the week, preferably during the evening on Wednesday. This ceremony is necessary for us to purify ourselves with smudging material, pray and share our thoughts during the week. Our wish is to strengthen our group's spirituality. You might consider it similar in nature to your Bible studies during the week."

The Chaplain answered, "I need to see the list of participants." So, Grey Bear used an inmate letter form to create a signup sheet for a talking circle to be held on Wednesday and nineteen brothers signed up. They decided that it would be a good idea to have the talking circle during evening recreation, after everyone got off work. Grey Bear received an ADOC inmate letter response from the Chaplain. It stated,

> "Talking circles are not scheduled unless ONE of the following is true: A volunteer is Present, [or] Sweat was canceled for that week and the talking circle occurred in Multi-Faith (Chapel) under the direct supervision of the Chaplain. This is the Senior Chaplain's response to your request. Chaplain."

Grievance Protocol

While Grey Bear was incarcerated, the following grievance procedure was in place with the Arizona Department of Corrections. The processes and policies may have changed since his release, but the reader will have a good understanding of the grievance process at the time.

In order to follow through with the grievance process, a prisoner must complete and submit a lot of paperwork. At the base level, an inmate is supposed to resolve the problem with the official or officer with whom they are having the conflict, in person. In Grey Bear's experience, however, at the base level, the official might resort to giving the inmate a ticket arbitrarily for refusing to follow an order or raise their voice at the inmate as an automatic response. It is much better to walk away, than to start a conflict in that moment with an officer.

Or, the inmate can write an official, factual inmate letter detailing the situation, devoid of emotion or exaggeration while providing a reasonable solution. This letter is an informal grievance to the CPO III Counselor or a security officer of higher rank, whose position is to help inmates settle problems and resolve grievances at the base level. But there is an unspoken rule to never write any paperwork for any reason, which works to the inmate's disadvantage.

The informal grievance process begins when the counselor contacts the officer against whom the complaint was issued and tries to find a resolution or justifies the officer's action with policy. It is never a happy experience. Officers despise grievances, and an inmate who writes one may end up with an invisible target on his back. After talking to the officer, the CPO III calls the inmate to their office to let him know the response to the informal grievance, and if there is a solution. If there is no solution, the inmate can elevate the complaint to the next level by completing a grievance form within five days of the informal grievance. A grievance coordinator will review the paperwork, find a statement in policy that justifies the officer's behavior, and writes a response.

Usually the response will summarize (sometimes inaccurately) the concern of the grievance, quote policy that protects the officer, and will sometimes find fault with the inmate writing the grievance. The process is then repeated by the inmate who completes a grievance appeal form, submits it to a grievance appeal coordinator, who in turn gives it to the Warden and Director who often don't review the paperwork themselves, but is completed by someone on their behalf. By the time a grievance is processed through the *kangaroo court,* the prison officials have quoted policy like it's *some kind of religion* for the administrators.

When Grey Bear was housed in a particular ADOC facility, he submitted an informal grievance against the prison librarian. He was making copies of legal work to use in his Rule 32 Post Conviction relief and some of the documents belonged to other prisoners who had similar legal situations. They had formed a coalition to help each other and when Grey Bear tried to make copies the officer/librarian told him that he was confiscating the paperwork and wrote a disciplinary ticket for doing other people's legal work.

First, Grey Bear spoke to his Correctional Programs Officer (CPO III), the *counselor* officer whose job it was to resolve disputes, regarding his confiscated paperwork. Then, Grey Bear submitted an informal grievance and waited for the disciplinary sergeant to call him to his office that week.

It turns out, the prison units were shifting prisoners between units at the time and Grey Bear was told he would be going to a new correctional facility, a private prison. The counselor at the private prison called Grey Bear into his office and handed most of the legal work that was confiscated from the previous prison, stating that the previous counselor was *insistent* that the paperwork be returned.

Grievances Filed

By June 2009, twenty-two Native Americans had turned-in informal grievances against the officers who had desecrated the sweat lodge. They threw a gigantic boulder into the lake and the waves it caused would become a backlash that hit them for years to come. In June 2009, Grey Bear received the following response from the Pastoral Activities Administrator:

> "This is in response to your attempt at Informal Resolution of the following: that the private prison staff desecrated the Native American sweat lodge during the unit search conducted on May 28, 2009 by conducting an unapproved search of the sweat lodge and surrounding area.
>
> Upon review of your complaint, I have discovered that a quarterly unit search was being conducted on May 28,

2009. The sweat lodge was searched as well. Before the search was conducted on the lodge and surrounding area of the lodge, the Warden, Deputy Warden, Chief of Security and Institutional Chaplain were notified.

The unit Chaplain was asked to monitor the search, to ensure that the provisions of Department Order 904 – Inmate Religious Activities were met. Section 904.4 of that department Order – Religious Accommodations, specifically section – 1.4.1.1.1. states: The lodge site and all associated areas are subject to search. Because the lodge and fire pit are sacred areas, searches of them shall be done only with approval from the shift commander and appropriate notification to the Warden Deputy Warden and the Chaplain.

I find that the requirements cited in Department order 904.4. were adhered to. The unit Chaplain was present during the search of the sweat lodge. His report to the Deputy Warden reflects that the search was conducted in a professional manner and the staff conducted themselves accordingly.

Based on the above information, your issues are resolved. If you do not agree, then you may elevate your complaint to the next level in accordance with Department Order 802 – Inmate Grievance System."

The other brothers in the circle received similar answers. The first weekend of June, Grey Bear brought a stack of grievance forms for the brothers to fill out. He told the brothers to write the same grievance as they did previously, which they did; some of them needed help with their paperwork. The second time, the brothers encountered several problems when submitting grievances.

First, Grey Bear was unfamiliar with the entire formal process at the new prison. Some of the brothers had copies of the grievance system from more than ten years ago, and while he made a copy from the prison library, the policy changed while the brothers were in the process of filing their grievances.

Next, Grey Bear's *bunky* asked to copy his grievance, but his *bunky* didn't return it on time, so Grey Bear missed the grievance deadline, along with half of the brothers. Thankfully, many of brothers stayed the course and their grievances were submitted in a timely manner. Grey Bear's failure would spur him to write three more grievances over the next two years regarding the overt retaliation that prison officials would *dish out* to the Native Americans. Some of the brothers who turned in grievances were summoned to the Central Disciplinary Unit (CDU) for their actions.

With classic *Gestapo-like* treatment, the brothers were interrogated and intimidated. One of the brothers was given a ticket for including *hearsay* in his grievance, because he wrote that the officer was dancing on the grounds. Grey Bear's brothers said that the officers were trying to determine if the Native Americans were going to sue the prison system for the sweat lodge desecration.

The *circle* decided not to have any more ceremonies until their Spiritual Advisor could visit, survey the extensive damage to the sweat lodge, and then help build and re-bless a new sweat lodge. However, negative feelings started to manifest for many of the Native inmates who saw the gaping hole in the sweat lodge as they walked past it every day. The sweat lodge had been a living force for the men.

Within the willow poles, the Native brother's hopes, prayers and dreams had been shared. The sweat lodge represented the Universe. They connected with the Creator and Mother Earth with its power. The sweat lodge was now dead. To see it in its desecrated condition tore at the roots of their hearts. So, at a second talking circle in June they decided to take down the sweat lodge and free its spirit. As a group, the inmates removed the ties from the willow poles, pulled them from the damaged earth and released them to the Great Spirit as the poles were placed in the sacred fire pit and burned.

When a sacred item is desecrated, or so old that it is falling apart, burning them is the Native American's way to release that item. The item's ash is given back to Mother Earth to return to the circle of life, while the spirit of the item flies skyward with the smoke to the Creator. Any negative energies imbued in that item are released as well. So, when the brothers released the sweat lodge, it was out of great respect for the Creator, Mother Earth and the inipi.

The prison officials didn't see it that way. In June 2009, the Deputy Warden met the pipe holder at the sweat lodge area, had him placed in handcuffs and taken to the CDU, also known as *the hole*. When an inmate was placed in the CDU, they were kept there for seven days or less, then returned to the general population. After seven days the pipe holder was still in solitary confinement. The brothers prayed that the prison administration would release their spiritual leader from the psychological torture he was enduring, but he was kept in the hole for forty days, then shipped to another prison.

Many knew Eagle, the pipe holder, as a person of great honor and sensibility. Some of the prison officers and teachers knew him as a kind and intelligent Native American spokesperson for the indigenous prisoners; so when he was given the *diesel* treatment (getting relocated to another prison), for standing up for their beliefs, the administration lost the respect of some of its officers.

From that point on, the prison officials at the private prison decided to wage an unspoken conflict against the Native Americans.

Results of the Grievances Filed

In June 2009, thirteen members of the sweat lodge circle were summoned to visitation for a meeting with the administration. Several members of the administration were waiting in the room, including the Warden, Deputy Warden and other prison officials. The officials announced to the Native Americans that a previously unenforced rule would now be enforced. The Native Americans were not allowed on their religious grounds unless a sweat ceremony was being conducted. If there was not enough wood to hold a sweat, the Native American prisoners would have to use the Christian chapel for a talking circle.

This rule, which was never enforced before, seemed like an another attempt to *Christianize* the Indians. Why were things changing now, after several years of open access to their sacred area? The Natives present at the meeting asked why they were being retaliated against. The officials denied that they were retaliating against them, but merely following rules that weren't enforced before. The timing was impeccable, as the Native Americans addressed the conflict regarding their religious boxes. They wanted to know why their rights were being violated during every search. The prison officials ended the meeting without providing an answer.

A few days later, maintenance workers welded the gates on the north and east side entrances of the religious grounds. The fence surrounding the Native American religious area was only three-foot high, but the gates on the fence were a symbolic gesture of oppression. The general inmate population and officers shook their head as they walked past the maintenance workers welding the gates. There was a padlock placed on each gate, even though an inmate could easily hop over it. For five years the *unit* had a sweat lodge and the sacred ground had been open for Native Americans to use for personal prayers, smudging and social gatherings for the spiritual members.

Since the Native inmates could no longer sweat, they were told that on Saturday they were going to be locked out of the sacred grounds. They were told to use the multi-denominational (Christian) chapel for their talking circle. The Native Americans had received the *inside word* from officers that the administration expected them to jump on to their religious grounds and protest. Security officers had the order to *cuff up* any Native American who set foot on their religious grounds.

Up to that point, there were rumors circulating between the officers and program workers about what was going on with the religious ground and the Native American's circle. Most of them were paranoid about who would be to be taken to the hole or interrogated. There were reports that members of the circle were closely scrutinized and issued unusual tickets (write-up for a policy violation). It was hard to keep track of the incidents because most of the brothers did not want their name *on paper.* That is, they were afraid to be retaliated against by the prison guards and administration for filing paperwork. They decided to *lay low,* not gather together and keep following through with the paperwork. Whenever Grey Bear wrote anything, he was paranoid; he felt as if the Deputy Warden was watching him on the security cameras. They all did. Although the incidents were minor, the group was intimidated.

So, on an overcast morning in June, the first Saturday after the sweat lodge was gated, the circle members woke up early and prepared for a ceremony. The guards in each building called the Native Americans for early chow so they could get to the ceremony by seven o'clock in the morning, as they always did. Having been warned to be ready for a protest, the security guards were alert and had serious demeanors.

Tensions were high, the security officers suspected the Native brothers might try to use the religious area despite the warnings. Any Native who entered the grounds had a guaranteed trip to the CDU and probably another prison. The tension between the administration, security, chaplain, and the Native American religious circle had reached its peak. The brothers made their move. They ate their breakfast in silence and when finished, each inmate exited the cafeteria quietly, separately.

The chaplain was waiting for the Native brothers to gather in the chapel next door, pray the Christian way like *good little Indians* and play their drum. No one showed up. Fifty Native American prisoners showed up for breakfast, fifty walked past the chapel without looking inside or entering. Instead, they looked across the empty yard to the hollow circle in the mud where the sweat lodge was located. The inmates felt the pain of hundreds of years of oppression. The sky was grey and the air was cold. Each man returned to their dorm; their protest was a silent one.

Later, the Sergeant on duty stopped by the chapel and when he stepped inside, looked around and found the room empty, devoid of anything but a shelf of bibles and two clerks, he asked, "How many Native Americans showed up?"

"None," they replied. The officer sprung a shocked look on his face and walked out of the chapel, quietly.

The response to grievances needs to be weighed in reference to the retaliation that an inmate may receive. Retaliation usually starts with excessive searches conducted by officials and their frivolous ideas of how the rules are being broken. Pick and choose the battles submitted through the grievance process. A grievance should be written in a respectful manner. Ask for help and find someone (another inmate) who is familiar and willing to assist with filing paperwork. In addition, be careful of the words spoken and actions taken, as the walls have ears. There is no such thing as privacy in prison.

GREY BEAR STANDS UP

No one really knows when the rights of the Native Americans started to disappear in prison, and it is extremely rare for Natives to stand up against the prison system. As a group, Native American prisoners have become accustomed to being repressed. If the Native tribes continue on the dark spiral of complacency, all hope will be gone. We will have lost the will to stand up for what is right.

And if the brothers and sisters will not stand up while in prison, they won't know who they are when they exit from prison. They will return into the darkness of urban cities and step away from the Sacred Hoop forever. So, this book is written to speak to all the brothers and sisters of Native America today and tomorrow, it is time to *stand up for our people!*

CEREMONIES, SACRED ITEMS AND RELIGIOUS FREEDOM

CHAPTER 1

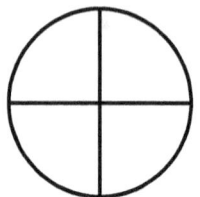

NATIVE AMERICAN SPIRITUAL BELIEFS

Native American Spirituality by Walks in Faith

To be a proud Native American is important; but to learn of my heritage, culture and spirituality, and apply what I've learned to my daily life is far more important to me.

In my trials and tribulations, I have applied my spirituality and faith and learned to call on the Creator for help and guidance. I rely on Him for peace and comfort, for strength and bravery, for wisdom and knowledge. One can say that these attributes can be found in all religions.

Who am I to say or believe that I know which is right and which is wrong? Or, who or what to believe in? I believe every man and woman must find their own way, and in their search, the Creator will find them, us. The calling.

I believe that Native Americans can grasp the religion of their ancestors with an open heart, spirit and mind. It is not pagan or witchcraft. It is nothing to be feared or judged, as so often is the case. The Native American's spirituality is widely misunderstood.

It *teaches me* to live and respect all things created by the Maker. It teaches me to walk the Red Road, which to the Christian's belief and faith, is the straight and narrow path. It teaches me to care for the people and land; to trust and have faith; to be kind to my neighbor; to be generous and protective; to be humble. How can anyone say that these things are wrong? Ask yourself.

I believe all religions that share these teachings are important to the race from whom they originated. For me, it is the Native American religion. I am Native American, and I believe.

Love, hope, balance, stability and courage. The Native American Way.

Native American Spirituality by Spotted Owl

I always wanted to go to a sweat lodge ceremony, but I couldn't find one. When I found the ceremony in prison, it was new to me. I've been *sweating* for the last twenty months, and have learned more than I could ever imagine about the sweat lodge, Mother Earth, the Rock People and the Winged One who carries the prayers and songs to the Creator. I now understand that all things are connected to each other.

The sweat lodge, water line, altar, the fire in the fire pit, the rocks in the fire, the water that is poured on the rocks, the herbs that are used, the pipe and the smudge sticks are all from Mother Earth. She provides everything for the people and the Creator provided Mother Earth for people to live on the land and watch over it. Native American spirituality brought me closer to Mother Earth, the Creator and all living things. It brought me closer to the Native Way. I wasn't taught the Native Way until incarceration.

Native American Spirituality by Grey Bear

We wander through the cities lost, always seeking, yet, never knowing. Native Americans are born in a gray world torn between darkness and light. One path ascends to Spirit Mountain, towering, surrounded by deserts, forests and clouds. The desert looks long and harsh and represents hardship. The forests are filled with the spirits of our ancestors and the mountain is nearly insurmountable. This path is a lonely one. To gain spiritual strength one must suffer; for others and for one's own self-release.

The other path, the easy way, spirals downward toward a dark lake. There are people smiling in the darkness, "Come join us in the darkness!" they beckon. There are no deserts of obligation or forests of responsibility to hinder you. We all travel downward sometime in our life. We get too close to the water, stumble and fall in. The people in the lake are drowning, pulling you under with them. The lake represents the cold, easy life. When we lose ourselves in this lake we drown in a dark abyss of laziness, inertia and addictions. The void of entropy.

In an environment of uncertainty, the sweat lodge is on the eastside of Spirit Mountain. The sweat lodge is part of the path leading upward. The lodge is the beacon of light that points the way to the will of the *Great Mystery*. The sweat lodge is a connection between Mother Earth, oneself and the Creator. When we walk onto the religious grounds, we walk back in time to our ancestors' *hogan, tipi,* or *long house.* The Great Spirit waits patiently as we prepare the grounds in a sacred manner. We bring our drum, gourd and voice into the sweat lodge. We crawl back into the womb of Mother Earth. The *Eternal Fire* brings heat and energy to the rock people. Entering the lodge, we are clothed in ignorance, bias, prejudice and all the lies we've accepted throughout the week. The flap closes and we shed them.

When we lose ourselves to the dark of the sweat lodge, we find ourselves in the middle of the universe, standing next to the Sacred Hoop. Anything we think we know is nothing compared to the wisdom of the universe. Water, a gift from Father Sky, is combined with the energy of the rocks to create the breath of the Creator, the hot steam shows how pitiful and lowly we are as humans. Only with humility can we endure. When we open our inner eye, we can see the beginning, the middle, the end and the birth of all things. We see the universe.

The flap opens and we crawl out reborn. A new beginning, a few songs closer to the Sacred Hoop. We sweat four rounds for the Four Directions. In these rounds we pray for the children, the women, the medicine and the Warrior Spirit, respectively. We take the pain of suffering and hardship on our own backs and pray for release from pain and fear. When we need help, we pray for each other. I hold my prayer shield over my brothers, and they hold their prayer shields over me, allowing our circle to intertwine into one great hoop shield of prayer. We find hope and direction.

In prison, where desperation persists in such a dark cold place, Native American spirituality brings us strength; it brings us to the Red Road toward redemption. The Red Road is also called the *Corn Pollen Road* or *Peyote Road,* depending on one's concept. The only rule we hold onto from one *flap* to the next is to be respectful, especially to all our relations.

First and foremost, we give respect to Grandfather, the Creator, the Great Mystery. *Tunkashila, Wakan Tanka* surrounds us with all that has been created. We give respect to Father Sky and Mother Earth. Father Sky brings the rain to Mother Earth who carries all life. All living things on this green planet are descended from the same place. Even the rocks are considered our ancestors. If respect is lost for the world in which we dwell, the world will be destroyed as a result. Our relatives understood all these precepts.

As Native Americans we are exposed to and assimilated into non-Indian culture, many lost their way. The American culture drew us away from the Red Road and taught us to be selfish and disrespectful to our ancestors and to others. The society that taught us negative values, habits and addictions calls us savages. Repeatedly, Native Americans are locked up in the prison system. The only way out is the Red Road, which is often blocked by the repressive acts of prison officials. Our way is often burdened.

But Native Americans are resilient. We have survived despite the genocide and oppression historically enacted on the Red Nation. We have survived because we strengthen one another. Our people each represent a part of a sacred circle, the Sacred Hoop that connects all things. Each one of us represents an important part of this world, this universe. It is for this reason we must be respectful of all relations, because we are each combined in spirit.

We respect the animals and winged ones as our older brothers and sisters. They have a deep connection to the spirit world and speak to and understand the language of Mother Earth and Father Sky. Sometimes they must translate messages to us from the Creator. Unlike humans, the animals do not judge or imprison one another. Each animal knows its place and never asks what it can get in return. The animals and winged ones are older, smarter. We are the young and the unknowledgeable.

When a Native American learns these things, they connect in harmony to all that is good. All that is good is the balance of life that gives our Nation strength from generation to generation. We strengthen the Sacred Hoop with our ceremonies and spiritual knowledge. In a prison setting there is much to gain from the sweat lodge ceremony, the pipe ceremony and the talking circle. These ceremonies should be conducted on Native American religious grounds, at the sweat lodge area. Private prayer should be allowed on the religious ground as well. ADOC policy in 2016, did not allow the religious grounds to be used for anything except a sweat ceremony.

The Native inmates have adopted intertribal customs. We call to the spirits with our offerings by smudging herbs, releasing corn pollen or offering a pinch of tobacco. We pray to the Four Directions, which represent the balance of all things. We pray upward for the Creator, downward for Mother Earth; then inward for our inner spirit, our true connection to the Great Spirit. There are different roads that lead upward. We respect that other religions have their own way. Our circles link to create one great circle around the incredible journey of life.

The Eagle soars to reach the mountaintop, its final journey. The Eagle passes onto the spirit world; its body returns to Mother Earth. Somewhere in the forest an egg hatches, a new eagle (eaglet) is born.

The Sacred Circle encompasses all things.

Prison Intertribal Traditions by Grey Bear

Every Saturday morning, we go to the sweat lodge area and enter the realm of our ancestors.

Native Americans from different tribes come together. Our prayers and songs unite to strengthen our Native Circle. One brother sings a Native American Church song, another sings song of the Hualapai, another sings Sioux. We adopt the traditional song and customs from many different tribes. We listen to each other's teachings and creation stories and blend together into one Red Nation, united spiritually. We don't say that one way to worship the Creator is the better than the other.

We connect with Natives from other circles of worship with our prayers. We connect with the sweat lodges and talking circles at other prisons and outside the walls. Our circles spread across the Tribal Nations and Mother Earth. With the strength of the Great Spirit we pray together.

We pray for the children of all nations.

We pray for the women of all nations.

We pray for the medicine of all nations.

We pray for the warriors of all nations.

We pray for the winged, the four-legged and the creepy crawlers.

We pray for the sweat lodge, Sacred Hoop and Sacred Pipe.

We pray for protection and healing for Mother Earth.

We give thanks for the Creator's blessings.

We do this for the Red Nation.

We do this so we can live.

We do this for all nations.

We are Intertribal.

CHAPTER 2

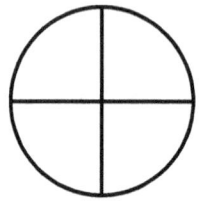

CEREMONIES

Introduction

According to Matthiesen, in 1881, the Sundance Ritual was forbidden on the Sioux reservations. Government agents had complained about *heathen* and *pagan* rituals interfering with the government's plans for Indian assimilation into white society. In 1883, the Courts of Indian Offenses were established on Indian reservations by the Secretary of Interior Henry M. Teller. All Native American religious dances were made illegal, including the Sun Dance, Scalp Dance and other religious feasts.

The punishment for breaking those laws was the denial of food rations from ten to thirty days. The denial of food rations was especially harsh since reservations had no access to food sources and scant employment opportunities. Also, the jails in those times had no definition of cruel and unusual treatment. Another part of the Indian Offenses declared that Indian Medicine Men who were caught practicing or sharing Native American religious rituals would be jailed from ten to thirty days for the first offense, and up to six months for any subsequent convictions of engaging in *barbarous rights and customs.*

Native American religious practitioners were forced to practice in secrecy. The Sun Dance ritual was held in secret locations. Non-Indians were regarded as outsiders on reservations. Native American spirituality went underground with the spread of *Peyotism* which resulted from the movement. The Peyote religion, known as the *Peyote Road,* became a positive way for Native Americans to cope with oppression.

Articles of Incorporation of the Native American Church (NAC) were drafted and agreed to by members of the Cheyenne, Otoe, Ponca Comanche, Kiowa and Apache tribes in Oklahoma on October 10, 1918. Historical documents show that peyote was banned by government agents as early as 1888 and the trend to ban its usage completely continued on through the 1960s and even as recent as 1990.

Local racist governments were given tremendous power to repress Indians with various laws; while on other reservations, Indians ignored the laws because government agents lacked the power to effectively enforce them. Government religious intolerance continued up through 1978 until the passage of the American Indian Religious Freedom Act of 1978. Overt Native American religious intolerance is still active in today's penological systems.

The Ghost Dance

In 1890, a Paiute Messiah named Wovoka brought good news to the Indians suffering from hardship through the Ghost Dance, a religion similar to some of the tenets of Christianity that the missionaries were preaching.

Wovoka preached to cause no harm to others and to always do right. The rituals included singing special songs and dancing in a circle at night, which would heal, help bring visions and cause changes in the natural world. The good news – learn how to Ghost Dance and the suffering the Natives were experiencing would turn around. The Great Spirit would bring back all the game (wildlife such as buffalo and deer), the dead Indians from the past would come back to life, and a great flood would remove white man.

Wovoka shared that if the Native Americans wore the sacred Ghost Shirt they would be impervious to bullets. Indians from many tribes traveled to meet Wovoka, the Indian Messiah, as he represented the return of Christ. The Ghost Dance religion spread throughout the reservations as a symbol of hope.

When the missionaries, reservation agents and newspapers heard of Wovoka, they overreacted and spread stories of dissent. Bureau of Indian Affairs agents, who were all non-Indian and had oversight over the different tribes, became alarmed. The reservation agent at the Rosebud reservation threatened to take away the Ghost Dancer's rations, while Crow, Brule and dancers in Minnesota were arrested. The Indian police and government troops tried to suppress the Ghost Dancers, but the Ghost Dance continued. Finally, the Bureau of Indian Affairs ordered leaders who were spreading the religion be arrested.

Sitting Bull was on the list of *fomenters of disturbances* for spreading the Ghost Dance. The soldiers who wanted him arrested, sent the Indian police to apprehend him, but there was an altercation during the arrest, and Sitting Bull was shot and killed on December 15, 1890.

When Chief Big Foot of the Miniconjou heard of Sitting Bull's death, he led his people toward Pine Ridge, South Dakota, to escape from the government troops who were coming to arrest him.

The soldiers intercepted the tribe on their way to Pine Ridge, made them camp at Wounded Knee Creek and surrounded the camp of three-hundred and fifty Indians. The next morning the soldiers started to search the camp for weapons when a gunshot was fired.

The soldiers used rifles and a Hotchkiss cannon on the unarmed camp of Indians, killing twenty-five of their own troops with *friendly fire*. Approximately, three-hundred Indians were killed, including Chief Bigfoot and two-thirds of the women and children, many of whom were hunted down while they were trying to flee. The dead Indians were placed in a mass grave. Later, twenty of the soldiers received the Congressional Medal of Honor for their actions.

In the years following the Wounded Knee massacre, all ceremonies on reservations were banned including the sweat lodge. By 1902, the Commissioner of Indian Affairs, W.A. Jones, urged for the end of all Indian practices including,

"...long hair, body paint, blankets, etc.," and to withhold rations from Indians who didn't comply.

Through the 1920s, the Hopi, Pueblo and Navajo Nations were the focus of oppression by the Commissioner of Indian affairs. The Indians were spied on by reservation agents who were either Christians or missionaries. The agents made many ludicrous claims about the inappropriateness of the dances, sometimes stating that they were sexual in nature when they weren't. In 1921, Charles Burke, Commissioner of Indian Affairs, targeted the Pueblo Indians' religious dance practice. He pushed for the enforcement of Indian Offenses against them and enacted regulations that required Indian boarding school students to attend Sunday school.

Burke had the reservation agents distribute letters that admonished the Indians for their religious practices. John Collier was a local non-Indian who was familiar with and respected the Pueblo's ceremonies. He advocated for the Indians before Congress and in 1934 was elected as the Commissioner of Indian Affairs. Collier overturned the regulations against Native American religious practices, but Native American religious intolerance did not end. Instead, it synthesized into land issues between the non-Indians who wanted to exploit the land, and the people who inhabited it first.

The Talking Circle Ceremony

The Talking Circle ceremony brings the Native American group together for smudging, purification, learning and healing. The Talking Circle ceremony should take place on the Native American sweat lodge grounds, as the area is sacred. The location is usually a designated area as it is important to have the ceremony outdoors in a prison setting because smudging with ceremonial herbs and bringing religious items are an integral part of the ceremony.

The Native brothers stand in a circle along with someone who has been designated as the Conductor. The Conductor of the talking circle smudges by giving an offering to the Creator, Mother Earth and the Four Directions, then the other attendees smudge themselves. The shell that holds the herbs is passed to the left and each Native smudges himself, then passes the shell and herbs *sunwise* (clockwise). When the shell returns to the conductor he or she places it in the middle of the circle, which allows the herbs to burn during the talking circle.

The Conductor says an opening prayer. After the prayer, he will speak to the group. He (or she) may have a specific subject for the group or may leave it open to the members. Moving sunwise each member of the group has an opportunity to speak or pass. If a drum or gourd has been brought, it is passed to each speaker who can sing if they desire. Once everyone has spoken or sung, the circle is completed as it returns to the Conductor who ends the talking circle with a closing prayer. The ceremony can last up to two hours depending on the number of speakers. On a rare occasion, it may be necessary to hold a short talking circle where only a few participants speak. This could happen if it starts to rain or if a talking circle is held before a sweat ceremony.

In prison, Native Americans can ask for a specific day during the week for a talking circle turnout, knowing that they should have equal access and opportunities to gather as other religions in prison.

The Pipe Ceremony

In an institutional setting, the pipe ceremony is similar to a talking circle, but the process is determined by the pipe holder and pipe carrier. Within the circle of Native American prisoners, there is usually one inmate who is designated as the pipe holder. This person is a Native American with a high moral standing and carries great responsibility by ensuring each ceremony is run properly. The pipe ceremony can be held in conjunction with the sweat ceremony or the talking circle.

The Native American people hold the sacred pipe with great respect and reverence. Only the inmate pipe holder, a Spiritual Advisor or designated prison official can handle the pipe. A provision for the pipe ceremony existed in ADOCs 1996 religious policy, DO 900/904,

> "1.5.4 Pipe ceremonies are religious ceremonies involving the use of the sacred pipe. The frequency and details shall be arranged through the Chaplain, in consultation with the Warden, Deputy Warden, Administrator or Chief of Security. 1.5.4.1 Pipe ceremonies, including smudging, shall only be conducted outdoors. Inmates who are in detention or a special management unit shall be allowed to conduct the ceremonies only during their regularly scheduled exercise time in an outdoor exercise area."

Unfortunately, this provision was also removed from policy in 1996. Without proper policy to have access to the pipe ceremony Native Americans may be arbitrarily denied the sacred pipe. However, as of 2016, the ceremonial pipe is now mentioned in ADOC policy.

Native Americans should be allowed to hold a pipe ceremony for holidays or special occasions, besides their regularly scheduled turnouts.

Pow Wow Ceremony

ADOC Policy from January 17, 1997, stated in section 900/904 1.5.5.,

> "Pow Wows (spiritual gatherings) are considered a closed religious ceremony (not a banquet) – limited to Native Americans, contract representatives and guest performers."

The policy also listed several requirements and referenced Attachment B in ADOC policy 904, which outlines the ceremony. Today, the Pow Wow has been removed from policy, although references to a special annual religious event exists in Attachment A in ADOC policy 904 in current policy. Pow Wow ceremonies need to be reinstated for incarcerated Native American religious practitioners in Arizona.

Having a Pow Wow ceremony in a prison requires a lot of coordination. First, the event needs to be approved by prison officials. The date and time for the Pow Wow needs to be determined and flyers announcing the ceremony need to be made. All aspects of the Pow Wow need to be approved including the guest list (family, friends and inmates), the Spiritual Advisor and the singers. Food authorizations and accommodations need to be planned, as well as the coordination of the equipment and seating needed for the ceremony.

To host a Pow Wow it takes money, so in the past, the Native inmates would receive donations from various sources inside and outside the prison. ADOCs policy about fundraising has changed over the years, making it difficult for any ceremony to be held in prison. When the Native inmates still had all their rights, the religious group could set up an account allowing them to pay for ceremony.

CHAPTER 3

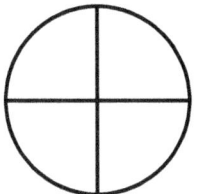

OVERVIEW OF CEREMONIAL AND SACRED ITEMS

Introduction

Native Americans in general are taught by their elders to regard all parts of this world as related entities. Since they are descended from Mother Earth and from Father Sky, all that exists is related. A characteristic of the Native American belief system is that we exist in a living universe. Were we not all related by atomic form? Aren't the Native American creation stories the closest thing to the truth to believing that the universe is a living entity and all it contains is related? Native people call the great truth, the *Great Mystery.*

The Creator encompasses all things that we don't know. Our Mother Earth is to be cared for and respected, for we are her children. We are brothers and sisters to all living things on this planet no matter how big or small, no matter how complex or simple. During the sweat ceremony Native Americans pray with heat from their ancestors, the rock people. The lava rocks *breathe* the Creator's hot breath upon the participants. The participants pray to the earth, air, water and to the *first,* for they are spirits who guide Native Americans, they are the Holy People, as the Diné recognize and practice.

Personification

Native Americans personify many objects. For example, a cloud may be a male or female, depending on its characteristics, and animals carry messages from the Great Spirit. All their religious objects act as spiritual reservoirs. They carry positive energies that can be strengthened with ceremonies or ruined through improper handling. If the item is improperly handled, it is considered desecrated, or permanently damaged. This is stressful to the Native American who spent time, energy and emotion to create a connection to the Great Spirit with his sacred items.

Prison Blessing

There are several ways an item can be blessed in a prison setting. The main and best way is for the blessing to take place during a sweat lodge ceremony; but a pipe ceremony or talking circle is also acceptable. A pipe holder or elder facilitating the sweat is the preferred person to perform the blessing. When an item gets blessed, a prayer is spoken to strengthen the item so it maintains it's positive energy. Once an item is blessed, it is activated until it becomes desecrated or is destroyed.

CHAPTER 4

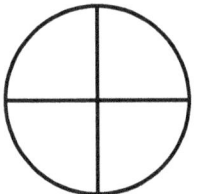

CEREMONIAL AND SACRED ITEMS

Introduction

All Native Americans should have access to sacred items and sacred areas because they help establish communication with all creation and with the Creator. The oppressive ADOC religious policy has been used to justify the sacrilege of Native American religious items and areas. There are only three ways an item can be desecrated and to reiterate what has been shared:

First, anyone who has bad thoughts or malice running through their mind or emotions will desecrate a sacred item if they touch it. It is okay if the carrier uses it to pray for the healing of his own negative emotions or to heal those of others.

Second, any non-Indian or non-believer in native ways who touches a sacred item can desecrate it. This explains why it's important for the Native American prisoner to be present for searches of his religious box. If a blessed item needs to be viewed, the Native can handle the item safely. During quarterly searches, inmates are removed from their dorm and not allowed to witness the search of their items. Unfortunately, this gives the officer conducting the search the opportunity to handle the sacred items, as he pleases, even if it is against Native American religious policy.

Third, religious items can be desecrated if a woman is menstruating and she touches an object. This belief is verified in the US Department of Justice *Inmate Religious Beliefs and Practices,*

> "Native Americans prohibit women from handling the pipe, or nearing the sweat lodge and other sacred objects during menstruation, because they believe that her menstruation-related energy overpowers the power of the sacred object."

This information cannot be found in the 2016 Arizona Department of Corrections policy.

Different tribes have different beliefs. Their respective beliefs may use various ceremonial objects, so it is important for the chaplain at any prison to understand and respect these differences. Unfortunately, past experiences have shown chaplains will follow the oppressive policy of the ADOC strictly and without regard for Native American religious practices. It is their job to follow the policies, but ADOC needs to be open to items that are used.

List of Native American Religious Items

The following list represents Native American religious items in Arizona. Different tribes have different traditions; for example, the Mohave tribe uses a large gourd rattle for Bird Song; while the Navajo use a smaller gourd with a kettle drum for Native American Church music, peyote songs and other traditional Diné songs. Some of the required Native Americans sacred items are in a *gray zone* of policy and are subject to approval at the whim of the administration.

Sometimes items may be approved by one administration to be contrabanded by the next. The chaplain has the only list of religious objects that are allowed, and it is not written in policy. The chaplain, property officer and administration create walls blocking Native Americans from receiving spiritual objects. Most of these items are listed in Rose Ann Kisto's *Native American Religious Manual* and the Bureau of Justice manual as well.

Sacred Pipe

The ceremonial pipe represents the Universe. The pipe is like a sacred altar and believed by some tribes that the bowl of the pipe represents the female powers and the stem represents male powers. Until 2013, there were no provisions in ADOC policy related to a sacred pipe. Therefore, obtaining one for the Native American group had to be *worked out* with the facility chaplain.

Headbands

Headbands represent the sacred circle of life and the Sacred Hoop. The headband may be blessed by a pipe holder, elder, or it's owner. The blessing infuses the headband with *good medicine* and positive energy which brings spiritual strength to the participant. Different colored headbands represent different aspects of the earth and creation.

Beadwork and Necklaces

Native Americans use beadwork to help create and decorate their religious items. Bead work is used as a spiritual connection to the living world. Beads made of natural substances were often used to decorate ceremonial instruments such as gourd rattles and sacred pipes. Beadwork is also used on traditional Native American *regalia* (clothes). Using items decorated with beadwork and wearing items decorated with beadwork helps to strengthen the spiritual medicine of a ceremony and shows a connection to tribal traditions.

A beaded necklace can be used to help strengthen a person's prayers in the ways indicated above, and there are several styles that may have an animal design that is connected to that individual.

The choker necklace is important to Native American ceremonial practice depending on the practices of the individual Native American. It is worn to strengthen prayers as well. They are made from large beads, plastic or bone. They are always blessed and care should be given to safeguard them from desecration, otherwise the item loses its strength to help with ceremonies. Currently, these items are restricted by ADOC.

Prison officials have contrabanded and seized beadwork from Native American religious practitioners. A Senior Chaplain made the statement in a letter to the Native inmates:

> "A beaded item is on the approved items list, but beads and supplies for doing beadwork is not on the approved items list. Only items used for religious ceremony are considered for addition. This office is aware of no religious ceremony involving beads or doing beadwork."

The *Arizona Department of Corrections Native American Services Program Manual,* states in part:

> "Native American Religious paraphernalia, construction materials, items used to construct and decorate religious paraphernalia are not to be called hobby or craft; beads, needles, thread, bees wax, beading looms, leather hide, sinew, and fur pelts. Also, medallions represent clan or tribal affiliation and personal vision. Necklaces or chokers made of beads, bone, shells, fur, leather and/or porcupine quills."

Porcupine quills are used for beadwork, but are restricted by ADOC.

Eagle Feather / Feathers

Eagle feathers are rare and sacred. These feathers should be treated with respect and protected by a *No Touch* policy. Unfortunately, Grey Bear has experienced several situations where correctional officers mishandled eagle feathers at the prison unit. Often, a search was conducted without the inmate present and the feather was removed from the religious box and left on a bed or desk, leading to the conclusion that the officers had picked them up and moved them.

Medicine Bag

Worn around the neck like a religious medallion, this bag carries prayers, hopes and dreams.

The medicine bag is a sacred item that can be desecrated, if handled improperly. The contents of the medicine bag are personal and have powerful religious value to the holder. The contents placed inside the medicine bag are determined by the owner and are often personal items, such as a picture of a loved family member or some type of object given to the holder of the medicine bag. The bag should never be touched by a non-practitioner of Native American religion. If it needs to be opened, only the owner should open it because the contents are sacred and personal.

Unfortunately, during searches officials have mishandled the medicine bag by opening it with their bare hands and dumping its contents on the bed; thus, desecrating the bag. When this mishandling occurs, the Native inmate needs to create a new medicine bag.

Animal Bones

Bones, claws and teeth of animals are kept as talismans; are blessed and should be regarded as sacred objects.

Fur

Fur is used to construct religious objects such as medicine bags and regalia. Currently, ADOC does not allow fur as a sacred item.

Seashell

Abalone and dentalium shells are used to hold smudging herbs. These are blessed, sacred items that are used in ceremonies such as the talking circle, sweat and pipe ceremonies.

Tobacco Ties

The name given to the small cloth bag that holds tobacco. The bag is closed with a drawstring, so the tobacco inside that is used as an offering doesn't spill out. Tobacco offerings can be for the Creator, a person or place. It symbolizes a prayer or offering by its maker.

Medicine Bundle

A medicine bundle are ceremonial objects that are kept together in a leather bag or wrapped in leather or cloth. The objects in the medicine bundle have a strong, sacred power that is used for ceremonies. Traditionally it gave spiritual power to the person who held the bundle.

Buffalo Skull

Kept on the sweat lodge altar, this sacred item represents Native American's connection to the natural world and to the Buffalo Calf woman, a symbol of Native American traditions and culture for the Lakota people.

Sacred Stones

Sacred stones hold energy, medicine or other powers. They can be used to help strengthen ceremonies, especially healing ceremonies.

Candles

Candles have been used in ceremonies as a connection to the spirit world. Sometimes they are used to connect with animal spirit helpers or to helper spirits. There are other uses for candles depending on the background of the user.

Religious Box

A cardboard box becomes a Native American inmate's religious box or bundle. These boxes are decorated with symbols so the bundle itself becomes imbued with the strength of creation. The officials who search these boxes view its contents as junk, so they dump the contents of the bag like a bag of trash. The Native American can *see,* while the official is *blind.*

The Native shows respect for all things, while the officials show no respect for the Native American's beliefs. When a quarterly search takes place, officials from the various departments join the search of an inmate's items along with the security officers. Often unknowledgeable of Native beliefs regarding religious items, the officials run their hands over the item(s), desecrating it; or they sift their fingers through the box and mishandle the contents.

When the Native American inmate returns to his bunk, he finds that his once sacred objects have been defiled. The sacred items are now infected with cultural ignorance. The sacred objects that the Native American used to connect with the Creator have become dislocated from the Sacred Hoop and the owner now has a deep sense of loss.

When the Native inmates complain about their religious boxes being desecrated, they are treated with indifference. Their grievances are ignored by the officers, chaplain and administration. Those who complain never remain at the prison unit. Some get shipped to the hole, some are sent to the next unit. Many Native Americans won't get a religious box because of the poor treatment of sacred items.

Hair Grooming

Native Americans should be allowed to wear their hair according to their religious customs. Long hair is a cultural identity of being Native American and is sacred to some tribes. For Grey Bear, cutting his hair only occurred as a symbol of mourning the loss of a loved one. Significant life changes or events can also be a reason to cut the hair. When the hair is cut, it is saved in a braid and is ceremonially burned with sage or sweetgrass.

Native Foods

When a Pow Wow ceremony takes place, it is important to include a traditional feast of Native American foods. No consideration was given to Native Americans to serve ceremonial foods on special occasions in the ADOC. Some traditional foods include corn, squash, wild rice and buffalo.

CHAPTER 5

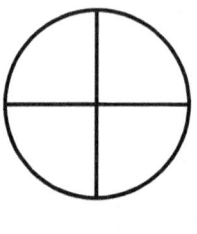

HERBS

Introduction

This chapter provides general information to the spiritual significance of each herb. There are many sources that can be researched to understand the unique traditions of Native American religious practices. Prison officials feign complete ignorance of Native American religious practices even though documentation from the Federal Bureau of Prisons guide and the ADOC manual were created to educate them. It is selective ignorance that leads to the prison's obstruction of Native American Freedom of Religious Exercise.

Grey Bear quickly learned how negative Arizona's Native American religious policy is toward the Indians. Following ADOC policy, he wrote a kite to the acting Chaplain requesting approval for the following Native American items: one abalone shell, one ounce of sage, one ounce of sweet grass, one ounce of cedar, one gourd, four bandanas, one medicine bag and one ounce of kinnikinnick tobacco.

The chaplains have a list of items allowed to Native Americans for their religious ceremonies and approval is needed. The items need to be ordered from an approved vendor in order to receive the items into *property* (Receiving Department). All the items were to be the smallest size possible and all herbs were limited to one ounce. The limitation on the herbs meant that Native inmates had to constantly re-order them, which can be an expensive and burdensome process.

Restricted Herbs

Herbs are a central part of Native American tradition. They are used as an offering to their Creator and is one of the many ways Native Americans establish their spirituality. Grey Bear's father, who was a bird singer (Medicine Man), taught him that when an offering is made to Father Sky, the Great Spirit, it's as if the person making the offering becomes a phone call from Mother Earth. The Native American breathes them, covers their bodies with the smoke and releases the herbs upwards to the spirits. Native Americans do not expect Christians to understand their traditions. They do not ask why books and chapters are in the bible. When herbs are denied to the Native American, it is like asking a Christian to remove pages from the bible.

The restricted sacred herbs allowed by ADOC are all non-narcotic, non-toxic, non-hallucinogenic and are legal substances. The chaplain's list included: sage, cedar, tobacco, creosote, sweet grass, kinikinnick, corn pollen, corn meal and corn husks. This limited list creates a major burden on Native American religion.

Many herbs that the tribes use are not on the list. The herbs on the chaplain's *approved items* list should also include other variations of each plant, but officials get technical with the list. Knowing that different tribes use a variety of herbs, essential herbs have been denied to Grey Bear for religious uses. Grey Bear has ordered these herbs, and when they come through the property department, they are not given to him and returned because the property officers are not trained to recognize that some herbs use alternative names. He was denied white sage, South Dakota sage, California Sage, Oregon sage and large leaf sage. Although Native American prisoners were supposed to be allowed to obtain sage from approved vendors, property officers didn't realize or want to know that the different names of sage meant the same thing.

Other herbs were denied because they were not on the list of approved items used by the chaplain. Some of the herbs that have been denied in Arizona prisons include anise seed, bearberry, corn meal, flag root, flat cedar, osha/snake root, lavender, peppermint, pinon, red cedar and spearmint.

Approved Herbs

The approved herbs by ADOC are limited. Some Native American prisoners seek to use other herbs inherent to their cultural teaching. The process to gain approval to use other herbs is onerous and discouraging. Prison officials and property officers arbitrarily deny Native Americans religious herbs.

Sage

Sage is one of the main herbs used in Native American Spiritual traditions. It is used outside a sweat lodge for cleansing, blessing and purification. There are many varieties of sage, but only *sage* is approved by ADOC for use by Native Americans. The problem that the Native inmates encounter is that approved vendors who send sage might use a more technical or descriptive name for plant than is on the chaplain's approved ordering list.

Using coffee as an example, the following explains how the name of an item creates a problem for Native American prisoners. The chaplain will sign the request for the Native American prisoner to purchase coffee. When the coffee arrives in the mail, the property officer reads the label that states *Columbian Coffee* or *decaffeinated coffee*. The wording is not specifically *coffee,* so it is denied. The same happens with sage that is ordered (See Restricted Herbs, page 167).

Cedar

Cedar is also used for cleansing, blessing and purifying. It is used inside the sweat lodge to consecrate it or make an item sacred. There are several variations of cedar, but only *cedar* is approved by ADOC. Cedar should mean any type of the many sources of cedar. However, flat cedar has been denied occasionally because the word *flat* has been included on the label, when most cedar is generally flat in nature.

Tobacco

Tobacco can be smoked, used in tobacco ties or a pinch of it can be released as an offering. Kinnikinnick is the most common mix of tobacco used in ceremonies and is a special blend of traditional herbs which include tobacco leaf. Kinnikinnick simply means *mixed* in the Algonquian language. Most Native Americans prefer to use the traditional kinnikinnick in ceremonies as a connection to tradition. The exact mixture will vary, depending on the location where the herbs are gathered or the tribal tradition. One of the main differences is that kinnikinnick is gathered and prepared using traditional methods, which is believed to strengthen the spiritual connection of the ceremony.

Sweet grass

This plant is available in a long braid and is used for cleansing, blessing and purifying. It is mainly used for smudging and is believed to bring positive, healthy energy to ceremonies. It is also used to clean away any negativity.

Corn Pollen

Corn pollen is used for offerings and prayer. For the Navajo, corn pollen represents the Holy People and is used to help continue the cycle of life. Native American prisoners struggle to find a source of corn pollen that can be sent to them through the rigorous approval system.

Corn Husks

Corn husks are often used for rolling traditional cigarettes with tobacco or kinnikinnick, which are used in ceremonies. Using a corn husk rather than a rolling paper establishes a better connection with tradition and strengthens the ceremony being conducted.

Creosote

Creosote is used like sage but is not approved for Native American ceremonial use by the ADOC.

CHAPTER 6

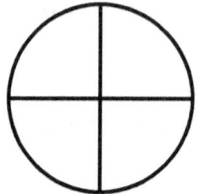

MUSICAL INSTRUMENTS

Music Program

During the time of Grey Bear's incarceration, the chaplains at the prisons used a music program to encourage prisoners to attend religious services. If a prisoner would attend two religious turnouts, then that prisoner was eligible to join the music program and practice and play a musical instrument of their choosing during a special time allotted to them. The problem was that only the Christian religious program at the prison had more than one turnout per week. So all Native American religious practitioners were ineligible because of their religion.

Concerning the ADOC music program, the rules and requirements can be flipflopped. Having an incentive to participate in a religious program is a violation of the establishment's clause (Lee V Weisman, 505 U.S. 577 (1992)) however, a claim under the establishment clause is rare in prison. A better claim would be under the Fourteenth Amendment under the constitution with *equal protection under the law.* The prison cannot treat one religious group better than another unless the reason is other than the belief itself, (Benjamin v. Coughlin, 905 F.2d 571 (2d Cir.1990)). For example, if one religious group gets a bigger room because they have more members than another group, then it is permissible.

During Grey Bear's incarceration, the music program was held in the religious chapel and overseen by the chaplain. According to the Establishment Clause of the Constitution, a government or government agency is not allowed to encourage one from being religious or following a certain religion. The ADOC music program was used as an incentive to practice religion. At one point it was required for an inmate to attend two religious turnouts per week, and since the Native Americans had only one turnout they were forced to attend the Christian bible study during the week in order to attend the music program. This ADOC policy has since been removed, but is an example to be remembered.

Native American Musical Instruments

Drums

The existence of drums as spiritual and traditional worship items may be as old a tradition as the sweat lodge. Drums are a central part of Native American religion. The drumbeat represents the heartbeat of Mother Earth and the Red Nation. It is important to have more than one drum to serve different purposes. There are no provisions for instruments in ADOC policy, causing difficulties in gaining approval.

Hand Drum

Made with a round wood frame, raw hide and sinew laces, the hand drum has a leather or raw hide cover stretched across a wood frame and is beaten with a drumstick. It varies in size from nine to eighteen inches and wears out because of being used regularly. It is used mostly outside of the sweat lodge.

Sweat Lodge Drum

A two-sided drum that works well in the sweat lodge and is designed to withstand the steam during the ceremony.

Pow Wow Drum

The Pow Wow drum is large and made for open air use. Constructed of wood and rawhide, it varies from twenty to thirty inches in size, but can be larger. Many players can gather around a Pow Wow drum and play it together, which increases their spiritual and social connection to each other and the ceremony.

Kettle Drum

Also known as a water drum, the kettle drum is central to Navajo traditions and the Native American Church. This durable drum sounds best in an enclosed space like a sweat lodge but works well outdoors also. The kettle drum has been contrabanded by the ADOC citing, "Native American leadership has been consulted on this issue but have never provided information relative to the importance, usage or physical characteristics of this item. Non-metal drums continue to be approved for use in group ceremony if available." The kettle drum is considered contraband by the ADOC.

Drumstick

When approval for a drum is obtained, be sure to also get approval for the drumstick. The drumstick is made of either wood or fiber glass with a leather or wool tip.

Personal Drum

Small drums are useful for private prayer and drum practice, and are usually eight to ten inches or smaller in size.

Other Drums

There are other styles of drums that are used by different tribes, including the Taos and Pueblo style drum. The variations of a drum are reflective of the natural materials available where the tribe is located, and the traditions passed down to build the instrument. Taos and Pueblo style drums are taller and two-sided.

Drum Storage

Large drums are usually stored in the chaplain's office or with the sweat lodge supplies. Small, personal drums might be allowed in the religious box. A drumstick should be kept with the drum.

Rattle (gourd)

There are different types of rattles for different tribal customs. Gourd rattles can vary in size; some tribes also use aluminum, rawhide and turtle shell for rattles.

Other Instruments

Flutes or other instruments may be part of a Native Americans traditional ceremony.

CHAPTER 7

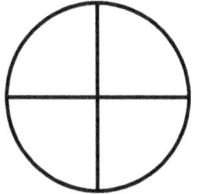

RELIGIOUS FREEDOM

In 1997, the Religious Freedom Restoration Act was struck down as being unconstitutional for the state courts. Without this religious protection, Native Americans lost case after case before 2000, due to the *penological* interests of *security* concerns. Native American religious freedom was lost, until the Religious Land Uses for Institutionalized Persons Act (RLUIPA) was passed in 2000, but the *system* had its own ways. Prison policies often lack the appropriate measures for Native Americans to practice their religion. Native American religious practitioners need advocacy to help them keep their religious freedom.

One recent example of this advocacy is the *Joint Submission to the U.N. Committee on the Elimination of Racial Discrimination Concerning Religious Freedoms of Indigenous Persons Deprived of Their Liberty in the United States of America...* Submitted August 1, 2014. This document was submitted by the non-profit agency Huy, which is an organization founded by Gabriel Galanda that "provides economic, educational, rehabilitative and religious support for American Indian, Alaska Native and other indigenous prisoners in the Pacific Northwest and throughout the United States."

The report was submitted jointly to the United Nations by The National Congress of American Indians, The United South and Eastern Tribes, Inc., The Round Valley Indian Tribes, The Sherwood Valley Band of Pomo Indians, The Penobscot Nation,

The Passamaquoddy Tribe at Sepayik, The Passamaquoddy Criminal Justice and Healing Commission, The Native Hawaiian Legal Corporation, The Native American Rights Fund, The National Native American Bar Association, The Indigenous Peoples Law and Policy Program at the University of Arizona James E. Rogers College of Law, The Indigenous Law and Policy Center at the Michigan State University College of Law, The Center for Indian Law and Policy at the Seattle University School of Law, The Indian Legal Program at the Arizona State University Sandra Day O'Connor College of Law, The American Civil Liberties Union, The American Civil Liberties Union of Washington and The Seattle Human Rights Commission.

This report concerned indigenous prisoner's freedoms to possess religious items, to participate in religious ceremonies, and to otherwise engage in traditional religious practices that are subject to an increasingly pervasive pattern of illegal restriction throughout the United States. The report uses several court cases in different states as examples of prisons unreasonably restricting Native American religious exercise. This report concludes with four recommendations:

> a. Immediately halt violations of indigenous prisoners' rights to freely exercise their religion;
>
> b. Instruct its Attorney General to undertake a comprehensive investigation of state laws and policies regarding indigenous exercise of religion;
>
> c. Engage indigenous communities in meaningful consultation to explore how federal, state, and indigenous governments may jointly develop and advance shared penological goals regarding incarcerated indigenous persons; and
>
> d. Provide any other recommendations the Committee considers appropriate.

The preceding report is an indication of the widespread problem of Native American incarceration. People who want to be active in positive change for Native Americans should work on reviewing and addressing the recommendations that have been presented. This book shows just the *tip of the iceberg* of the widespread difficulties Native American prisoners have and encounter while incarcerated.

CHAPTER 8

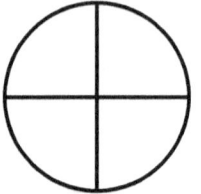

HISTORY OF NATIVE AMERICANS AND THE PRISON SYSTEM

Introduction

Religious freedom, missions, boarding schools, prison and religious oppression are all woven in the same blanket. In order to understand the intricate power of the system one must understand its history and actions. The great dark shadow of the American penological system is a black hole that is inherently *evil*. Evil is an opinionated term. There are many people who profit from the system and believe it is *good*. Whatever your stand, the origins of the system are rooted in religion and the perceptions of good vs. bad; and ultimately master vs. slave, or superior to inferior.

The Anglicans of Virginia and the Puritans of Massachusetts established colonies in North America in 1607 and 1620, respectively. Pilgrims had escaped the religious persecution from the Church of England. Their colony, the Massachusetts Bay Colony, had a government heavily influenced by its own church. Ironically, this colony did not tolerate dissent and banished a colonist named Roger Williams. Williams then founded Rhode Island with religious freedom as a premise.

Various colonies were founded throughout the east coast areas of Carolina, Maryland, Delaware, Pennsylvania and Rhode Island. The 1997 Supreme Court case, City of Boerne v. Flores,

521 U.S. 507, shows the first American legal document to use the term free exercise existed in an agreement between Lord Baltimore and the new Protestant Governor of Maryland, in order to not disturb the Christians and Roman Catholics in the *free exercise* of their religion. Also, in 1649 the Maryland assembly passed the Act concerning Religion stating in part,

> "[N]o person...professing to believe in Jesus Christ, shall from henceforth be any way troubled, molested, or discountenanced for or in respect of his or her religion nor in free exercise thereof . . . nor any way compelled to the belief or exercise of any other religion against his or her consent, so as they be not unfaithful to the Lord Proprietary, or molest or conspire against the Government."

The Rhode Island Charter of 1663 also protected religious freedom, but was stated in a different manner. Other agreements in Carolina, New York and New Jersey guaranteed religious freedom using language similar to the Rhode Island Charter during this period.

The purpose of the free exercise clause was to protect religious freedom as an *essential liberty.* A government could not hinder or try to influence a person's free exercise of religion unless there was a significant stated interest at conflict. It should be noted that the different religious groups that were recognized for the free exercise clause were all Christian based. Native American religious practice was either seen or thought of, as nonexistent or regarded as devil worship.

Boarding Schools

In the 1800s, government reservation agents working with tribes were often members of bible-based organizations. The agents were in charge of managing the Indians interests and assimilating them into white society. They helped to establish boarding schools and missions for the Indians. Indian children were forcibly taken from their parents and usually sent to schools with military type conditions that were purposely located far from their homes. Siblings were often separated and sent to different schools. The Office of Indian Affairs, which would later become the Bureau of Indian Affairs opened the first government boarding school in 1860. Federal officers were given the power to take children away from families in 1891.

According to the National Native American Boarding School Healing Coalition, there were twenty thousand Native American children attending boarding schools in 1900. By 1925, there were 60,889 Native American children in these boarding schools according to the Coalition. A year later, eighty-three percent of the school age children were attending boarding school.

In 1879, the Carlisle School was established in Pennsylvania by a former Civil War veteran, Henry Pratt. The school motto was to *kill the Indian and save the man.* Upon entering the school both Native boys' and girls' heads were shaved. The boys were forced to keep their hair short and the Indian children were forced to assimilate to white customs. By 1900, over one-hundred boarding schools were placed on or near reservations throughout the US. According to Utter, about sixty of the boarding schools were run by Protestant and Catholic groups until 1987. And parents weren't allowed to have a choice in their children's school placement until the Indian Child Welfare Act in 1978.

The children were forbidden from speaking their native languages. Punishment for speaking Indian and other infractions were whippings (with a lash or paddle), denial of rations, extra chores and solitary confinement. Indian children were coerced or forced to attend weekend Christian services. When the children turned eighteen years old, they could return to the reservation; but they did not speak their native tongue and were unknowledgeable of tribal customs. Many of the children who returned home were psychologically traumatized.

Some had difficulties adapting to their native culture, while some wandered to the cities where they assimilated into white society. Some ended up lost in alcoholism and panhandling. There are stories of Natives who returned from the boarding schools and were never able to adapt or be accepted. Some of the children died from diseases like tuberculosis and have never been accounted for.

The Indian Education Act of 1972 and the Indian Self Determination and Education Assistance Act of 1975 changed the way schools were operated; but some say the boarding school mentality still exists in reservation schools.

Native American Religious Rights Denied

Native Americans have revered mountains, geographic landmarks and locations as being sacred to their religious practices. In Badoni v. Higginson 455 F. Supp. 641 (D. Utah 1977) and Badoni v. Broadbent 452 U.S. 954 (1981), Navajo medicine men and tribal members tried to assert that the government caused major damage to the Navajo's holy area at Rainbow Bridge National Monument by allowing the Lake Powell, Arizona reservoir to rise and flood sacred ground.

The Diné were unable to perform their traditional ceremonies and tourists were allowed into the area. The court stated that the Navajo had no property rights to the area, although it was within the Navajo reservation, because it was held in federal ownership as a national monument after 1910. The public's *property rights* were given more weight than the Navajo's religious rights.

The Cherokee also lost a similar claim (flooding of their religious area) under similar circumstances in Sequoyah v. Tennessee Valley Authority (1980). The court stated that the claims were based on cultural values rather than religious values, even though the court also noted that the land was *sacred* to the Cherokee.

In the Hopi Indian Tribe v. Block and Wilson v. Block cases, the Hopi tried to fight development of the government-owned Snow Bowl ski area in Flagstaff. The Navajo and Hopi tribes regard the San Francisco Peaks to be sacred. The Navajo believe that the peaks are the body of a spirit being, while the Hopi believe that the Kachina beings live on the four peaks. Any type of development on the sacred mountains would hinder the Native American deities and, in turn, affect the people. The Wilson

Court was cited from the earlier decision in the Cherokee Sequoyah case and the Supreme Court ruled against the Indians.

The Lakota Sioux and Tsistsista tribes, in Crow v. Gullet, would lose their case trying to protect Bear Butte from developmental desecration in 1982. The AIRFA (American Indian Religious Freedom Act) did nothing to protect sacred Indian land. The court used the Hopi case as a reference to deny relief from injustice.

In 1988, the cases Lyng v. Northwest Indian Cemetery Protective Association and Employment Division v Smith would synthesize to seriously impair religious freedom. AIRFA was rejected in both cases. In the Supreme Court Lyng decision, Judge Sandra Day O'Connor claimed that ruling for the tribe's claims would create *religious servitudes* of federal land. The American Jewish Congress, the Christian Legal Society and the American Civil Liberties Union filed amicus briefs, a document filed on a court case submitted by a non-litigant, on behalf of the Indian's side. With religious freedom lost, the Lyng decision held major consequences for future cases.

Courts would refer to the Lyng case in rejecting other Native American free exercise of religion cases. United States v. Means (1989) involved using part of the Black Hills forest for a Native American religious cultural area. Attakai v. United States (1990) involved the Navajo – Hopi Settlement Act. The court in these cases referred to the Lyng case decision, using the terms religious servitude and *defacto beneficial ownership.* The Havasupai Tribe, north of the Colorado River Indian Reservation, tried to enjoin the US Forest Service from digging a uranium mine on sacred land. The court again ruled for the government's use of *its land.*

These cases spurred backlash from Native American tribes and religious groups who had interests in protecting the free exercise of religion. Cases involving Native American prisoner rights were often influenced by the Supreme Court's decisions made during the late 1980s through the early 1990s. Up through 1949, prisoners didn't have many rights. Little was known about the religious liberty of incarcerated Native Americans until the Native American Rights Fund started the *Indian Corrections Project* in 1972.

During the 1960s and 1970s advocates like Martin Luther King Jr. and Malcolm X brought to light the problems of blight and poverty in urban ghettos and black communities. Activists from Native American communities like Dennis Banks and Russel Means pointed out similar conditions on Indian reservations and discrimination with the government's assimilation programs. President Lyndon Johnson reacted by starting a *War on Poverty* to fix the social conditions that minorities faced when placed in substandard environments with substandard chances to improve their conditions.

Native American prisoners today are in constant need of support. Court cases are still being fought in the judicial system today that concern Native American prisoner's legal rights. *Prison Legal News* (PLN) has published several articles regarding Native American prisoner's religious rights. PLN reports that three Native American prisoners in Texas recently won a lawsuit to wear long hair in U.S.D.C. (S.D. Tex.), Case No. 2:12-cv-00166, 2019.

There have been many cases where Native American prisoners have filed court cases to recover their religious rights. For each case that has been filed, there have been hundreds who have suffered in silence from spiritual oppression.

GREY BEAR STANDS UP

Every year our religious rights disappear from policy. Prison administrators remove and restrict Native American religious practices and ceremonies in response to our requests for equality. If we don't stand up for ourselves, one day there will be no sweat lodge, one day there will be no pipe, one day there will be no drum. In the 1990s Native American prisoners and spiritual advocates testified before Congress for our rights. In 2020, we are worse off today than we have been for a long time. Native Americans in many states have few, if any rights for their religious practice.

As I walked into the second prison, my vacation into American slavery, the correction process, I did not really know where I was spiritually in my life. The forest had been burnt down and the animals roasted. A new facility for Big Brother had been built and the Native Americans eventually were given a spot to have their Sweat Lodge, smack dab in the middle of the recreational yard, which is a major walkway within five feet of our religious area. The area almost seemed like a stage for everyone to watch. Native American inmates at the unit once were free to use the sweat lodge ground during their recreation time for private prayer, gathering together, and to help assist the sweat lodge porter maintain the Native Americans' sacred religious area. This all ended when the Native Americans at the prison decided to stand up for their rights and the prison system retaliated. Watching the event unfold gave me a glimpse into an ominous future.

COURT CASES

CHAPTER 1

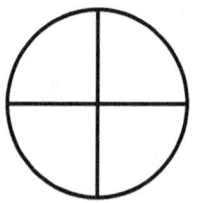

COURT CASES

Introduction

Native Americans have lived on the American continent without ever building a single prison. Along with disease epidemics and mass genocide, Europeans brought the penological concept to North America; and Native Americans were the first people on this continent to be imprisoned. Entire tribes were imprisoned. Many Native Americans were forcibly removed from their ancestral homelands and placed on reservations to make room for colonists and settlers.

The United States outlawed Native American religious practice. Children were taken from Native American parents and placed in boarding schools where Native American spiritual practice was abolished. After decades of abuse, nearly all Native Americans have felt the pain of intergenerational trauma. Reservations are mired in complex social problems that stem from unemployment and lack of education. Virtually all Native Americans have had family who have been incarcerated or have been trapped in the *justice* system.

The Intertribal way in which the Arizona Native inmates practice their faith was influenced by the teachings of different tribes and the Native American Church. Great walls stand against Native American religious practitioners that keep them from having the ability to stretch their wings as spiritual people. This chapter will show documented court cases that have affected Native American rights.

The Discovery Doctrine's Effect on Native American Rights

The *Discovery Doctrine* was the belief of European colonizers that since they were the first Christians to discover the land only traveled on by *heathen* Indians, the Christian colonizers could take possession of the land with no regard for those who were there first. The only way the Native Americans retained possession of any land was when they signed treaties that acknowledged their prior possession of it. Later, white man would coerce the Indians to alter the treaties to the white's benefit. The discovery doctrine became part of the American legal system in the case Johnson V. McIntosh.

Supreme Court Chief Justice John Marshall commented in Johnson v. McIntosh, 21 U. S. 543, 576-77 (1823) that from 1496 the King of England wished to send Christian explorers *to discover countries then unknown to Christian people, and gave them the right to take possession, notwithstanding the occupancy of the natives, who were heathens, as noted by Duthu. Also, he said the Indians were fierce savages... whose subsistence was drawn chiefly from the forest. To leave them in possession of their country was to leave the country a wilderness.* The ruling extinguished the land ownership rights of the Native Americans who inhabited America first. This decision set the context for other cases involving land rights for Native Americans.

Court Cases and Native American Religious Freedom

Before 1987, the legal base and the legal wording that protected religious freedom was first exhibited in the Supreme Court cases Sherbert v. Verner 374 U.S. 398 (1963) and Wisconsin v. Yoder, 406 U.S. 205 (1972). The legal reasoning: in order to cause a substantial burden to religion with a law or regulation, a government must prove that it has a compelling governmental interest and was using the least restrictive means to further that interest.

Turner v. Safely, 482 U.S. 78 (1987), was the first *domino* to fall that weakened prisoners' constitutional rights. The legal basis in this case stated,

> "When a prison regulation impinges on inmates' constitutional rights, the regulation is valid if it is reasonably related to legitimate penological interests."

From a Native American prisoner's viewpoint, *reasonably related,* seems to include racial discrimination and religious intolerance. From Grey Bear's perspective prison officials don't believe they need to give a reason as to why they denied a written request or contrabanded religious items, even though federal law states they are supposed to give a reason.

A week after the Turner ruling, the Supreme Court created an exception from the *compelling government interest* for cases involving religious freedom as determined in the case O'Lone v. Estate of Shabazz, 482 U.S. 342 (1987). In this case, Muslim prisoners were prevented from attending a weekly Jumu'ah service. Prison officials were able to oppress religious liberty by stating that the restriction was *reasonably related* to penological interests.

Martin Luther King Jr. once made the statement,

> "Injustice anywhere affects justice everywhere."

If Native American prisoners are suffering from the bitter cruelty of religious intolerance, other minority religions are also suffering. The domino effect of the *reasonably related* test (comparison) spread to the Lyng and Smith cases, resulting in the nationwide disintegration of religious rights.

In Lyng v. Northwest Indian Cemetery Protective Association 485 U.S. 439 (1988), members of the Yurok, Tolowa and Karok tribes tried to stop the US Forest Service from building a road through sacred land. Tribal members asserted that the destruction of sacred land from construction through the forest would violate their First Amendment, as the tribal members used the area for prayer and gathering resources used for religious purposes.

The court ruled that the tribes failed to show legal burden that coerced or penalized them for their beliefs. This case limited

Native Americans ability to protect their sacred site from the destruction of the construction of a road, and thereby destroying it; an area that was considered sacred by several Native American tribes. According to Echo-Hawk, the Lyng decision and other cases "stripped all Native people – and especially Indian prisoners – of the ability to defend their right to worship from unnecessary government infringements."

It should be noted that the American Indian Religious Freedom Act didn't help with the Lyng case. It did not help with the case Standing Deer v. Carlson 831 F. 2d 1525 (9th Cir. 1987) in which the courts stated,

> "(Regarding AIRFA) The Statute is *clear on its face* (it can be plainly seen). Nothing in its language indicates that it creates a procedural obligation on the part of government officials to consult with members of the Native American community before implementing rules of general application."

In other words, the AIRFA statute does not do anything, such as require a prison to protect religious rights any differently with or without the statute.

In the Employment Division, Department of Human Resources of Oregon v. Smith case, two Native American employees at a drug and alcohol rehabilitation center were fired for using peyote during a Native American Church ceremony and were denied unemployment benefits.

The employees entered a suit to challenge whether the controlled substance law was constitutional since the peyote was used as part of a religious ceremony. The Oregon Supreme Court ruled in the Native American plaintiff's favor; however, the US Supreme Court reversed the decision in 1990 sending religious freedom into the dark ages.

In the case Iron Eyes v. Henry, 907 F. 2d 811 (8th Circ. 1990), regarding Native American religious belief with hair length, was lost because of the Smith decision. This case was lost because of the bad precedents set in the Supreme Court.

And US v. Boyll, 774 F Supp. 1333, 1340 (D. NM, 1991) app. Dism'd. 968 F.2d 21 (10th Cir., 1992)

> "There can be no more excessive entanglement of Government with religion than the Government's attempt to impose a racial restriction to membership in a religious organization. The decision as to who can and who cannot be members of the Native American Church is an internal church judgment which the First Amendment shields from government interference."

Cases regarding religious rights were immediately impacted. In Yu Vang Yang v. Sturner, 750 F. Supp 558 (D.R.I. 1990) the court reversed an earlier decision that upheld a Hmong religious objection to autopsy because of the earlier decision in the Smith case (RFRA). Also, at hearings for the enactment of the Religious Freedom Restoration Act of 1993, Reverend Oliver S. Thomas, a representative of the Baptist Joint Committee on Public Affairs and the American Jewish Committee stated,

> "Since Smith was decided, governments throughout the US have run roughshod over religious convictions. Churches have been zoned even out of commercial areas. Jews have been subjected to autopsies in violation of their family's faith ... In time, every religion in America will suffer" (RFRA 1993).

In the *Study of Native American Prisoner Issues,* 1996, Walter Echo-Hawk explains that the Smith decision had affected other court decisions concerning Native American religious freedom. A prior decision in Teterud v. Burns, 5222 F2d 357 (8th Cir. 1975) protecting Native American religious belief had to be overruled.

Courts have criticized the imposition of ethnic criteria on inmate eligibility to practice Native American spirituality. See Combs v Correction Corp. of America 977 F. sup. 799, 802 (W.D. La., 1997),

> "[R]estricting the practice of the Native American Religion only to those prisoners of Native American

ancestry...offends the constitutional right to practice religion of one's choice."

In the 8th Circuit, the Missouri Appeals court affirmed the denial of a sweat lodge based on prior case law. In Fowler v. Crawford, 534 F.3d 931 (8th Cir. 2008), cert. denied. RLUIPA and the Religious Freedom Restoration Act failed to protect Native American religious freedom.

In more recent cases, results have been mixed. In Kinslow v. New Mexico Corrections Department (2009), Jimmy Kinslow, a Potawatomi tribal member, filed a federal lawsuit to get adequate time for sweat lodge access and traditional materials for his medicine bag. He won his suit under the First Amendment, the Religious Land Use and Institutionalized Persons Act (RLUIPA) and under New Mexico's Religious Freedom Restoration Act. This was in the 9th Circuit.

Native American v. Native American

Spotted Tail was a notorious figure during the Indian Wars of the 1800s. He was a Brule Sioux Chief who rode with Crazy Horse, Red Cloud and Sitting Bull. His cousin, Crow Dog, killed him August 5, 1881 and some believe that it was because Spotted Tail cooperated with the whites by selling sacred land in the Black Hills of South Dakota; others say that the issue was over a woman in the Crow Dog family.

The Brule resolved the murder in the traditional way, by ordering compensation to be given to Spotted Tail's family and exiling Crow Dog, who retired to a home he called Crow Dog's Paradise. The white public, however, demanded *justice* and Crow Dog was sentenced to be hanged in a Deadwood circuit court in the North Black Hills. Crow Dog was allowed to return home and prepare for his death, but the Supreme Court, in ex parte Crow Dog overturned his conviction, giving jurisdiction to the tribe. "I rode one hundred and fifty miles for nothing!" was Crow Dog's reply.

This led to the Major Crimes Act in 1885. Crow Dog's family was exiled for four generations.

American Indian Movement

In 1968, Clyde Bellecourt, Eddie Benton Banai, George Mitchell and Dennis Banks founded the *American Indian Movement* (AIM). National attention of AIM was boosted when they participated in the takeover of Alcatraz from 1969 to 1971. AIM would unify Native American people in many struggles during those years, including resisting the corporations that tried to exploit Indian reservations.

Russell Means, who would later become the spokesperson, joined AIM in 1970. The leadership needed a spiritual foundation, and Leonard Crow Dog, the great grandson of the Crow Dog who killed Spotted Tail, became the religious leader of AIM. He spread the teachings of the Sun Dance Way and Native American Church throughout the AIM movement in the 1970s. Native American tribal members from all nations were exposed to these practices.

Throughout the 1970s Native American prisoners started to fight for their religious rights. Many of the initial cases involved hair length. Once Native Americans won the right to have sweat lodges, Native American prisoners in Arizona depended on the guidance of spiritual advisors like Lenny Foster and Rose Ann Kisto. Different prisoners in different states had to find their way to learn Native American spirituality.

Unfortunately, Grey Bear was told many times that while he was standing up for Native American religious rights, to stop what he was doing by prison administrators and by Native Americans. He was told that fighting for their religious rights will have little effect in the grand scheme of things and that prison court cases don't affect *people outside of prison.* But, he believed (and still does) that standing up for Native American rights in prison, was and is important for Native American rehabilitation.

Headbands in the Courts

There is an ongoing conflict in the legal system concerning Native Americans having the right to wear headbands. 2016 ADOC policy regarding the use of headbands states that Native Americans are only allowed to wear a headband during a religious ceremony or in their own area for private prayer; not around the prison yard. Officers have been known to misinterpret private prayer and told the Native American to remove his headband. People often don't understand the significance of headbands for Native Americans. The headband was a part of a Native Americans sacred regalia, like a yippa cap to a person who is Jewish. This regalia was to be worn during most activities, including eating.

In the 1984 case, Reinert v. Haas, prison officials banned headbands because they believed that headbands promoted gang affiliation and other inmates would want to wear headbands. The court decided that no *compelling security interest* justified the band. In this case, the district court found,

> "Indian religion and Indian culture are one and the same. It is a way of life that is practiced constantly. Its essence, as a way of life, is living in harmony with all of one's surroundings. The circle is highly significant in Indian culture and religion, and this significance is expressed in the *cosmic circle,* a visual representation of basic forces of life and the universe. The headband is a symbol of the cosmic circle; however, the headband is not just symbolic, it is sacred."

In the 1987 case Standing Deer v. Carlson, the courts deferred to the prison officials concerns that headbands shouldn't be worn in the cafeteria because of security and sanitation concerns, although they could wear their headbands elsewhere around the yard.

Injustices

There is a disconnect that exists between Native Americans, their families, their tribe and the prison system. Many inmates don't have resources available to help them stand up for their rights. When they do try to stand for equal treatment, they experience endless retaliation from prison officials. When kites and grievances are written, prison officials have warned them about reduced time for their sweat ceremony.

The majority of Native Americans at any prison just want to do their time, have the freedom to practice their religion and not face problems from staff. Comparing ADOCs religious policy in 1994 to its policy at the end of 2010, prison officials in Arizona have swept away Native American rights while they were sitting in the sweat lodge. They lost their talking circle, pipe ceremony, beadwork and kettle drum. The only way these rights will be returned is through litigation.

But that is not enough. Even if they did win the return of some of these rights, prison officials will play the same game again. The Native American inmates start over, weaker each time until they no longer know who they are as people. With few rights for Native American prisoners as a basis for their religious practice, it is impossible to gain equality. They have been bullied into submission so long, the warrior spirit is hard to find. The Native inmates tell each other not to write kites or *stir up the water,* because prison conditions will get worse if they try to stand up for their rights. Conditions are already worse, brothers and sisters. As Native Americans, Grey Bear and *his relatives* knew that they needed to open their eyes and know their stance. If they didn't act now, there would be nothing left to fight for.

Native American Prisoner Advocacy

In the 1970s, there was little information on Native American prisoners. The only organization in the nation that addressed Native American prisoner issues was the *Navajo Nations Corrections Project.*

The Native American Rights Fund (NARF) was incorporated as a nonprofit organization in 1971 and this organization has documented Native American prisoner's rights. NARF is a major legal advocate for Native American tribes, and they have represented many of them on various issues.

The Native American Rights Fund started a project to address Native American prisoner's issues from 1972 – 1981. NARF stood before the Senate Select Committee on Indian Affairs in 1978 to support the American Indian Religious Freedom Act.

NARF found no organizations that paid attention to prisoner issues on a national level, and that few existed within the states. According to Joel Williams in the article, *American Jails,* the movement to gain Native American religious rights started in Nebraska in 1972, with a lawsuit to protect the long hair of several Native American prisoners, since cutting it would be a violation of their religious beliefs.

In 1995, the National Native American Prisoners Rights Advocates Coalition (NNAPRAC) was founded as a group of representatives to address Native American prisoner's issues. According to Walter Echo-Hawk, due to advocacy on behalf of Native American prisoners, from 1970 – 1987 litigation was successful in protecting the religious rights of Native Americans.

The rulings in the O'lone v. Estate of Shabazz, the Turner and Lyng cases caused a major weakness of court protection for Native American religious rights. Because of the effects of these decisions, many advocates testified before Congress in 1992 and 1993 at the Senate Indian Affairs field hearings in several different states. The testimonies showed a lack of adequate protection for the free exercise of Native American religion.

In 1996, Walter Echo-Hawk, an attorney for the Native American Church of North America and NARF drafted the *Study of Native American Prisoner Issues* for the National Indian Policy Center.

Religious Freedom Restoration Act

The passage of the Religious Freedom Restoration Act of 1993 and the Religious Land Use and Institutionalized Persons Act in 2000 restored the *compelling interest* test and *least restrictive means* test that protected religious freedom in state and federal prisons. The compelling interest test for prisons involves their ability to restrict a practice if it is in the interest of safety and security for the prisoners. The *compelling interest* would be safety and security. With RLUIPA, a prison regulation must not cause a substantial burden on inmates' religious rights unless it is done in the least restrictive way. Least restrictive means that the practice should be allowed unless it violates security or safety. Some states adopted these tests in their own statutes.

Arizona was one of the states to have these tests. However, the Arizona Department of Corrections lacks a policy that protects Native American religious practice to its fullest. The security officers must enact their own unwritten policy based on respect, similar to the oral tradition that Native Americans have followed for centuries.

The officers had to tell each other not to touch the medicine bag, eagle feather and sacred items of the Native Americans because the written policy is deficient. Not every officer was educated to these things however, and conflict was the result of officer's miseducation. There were ways that security had looked out for the religious protection of the Native Americans, but this was a precarious balance that easily could go in the opposite direction.

Case in point, after the Senior Chaplain removed the water drum from the Native American inmate's ceremony, the Chaplain eased the noose around their necks and then moved to another prison. The new Chaplain had been helpful, but the policy was still in the *dark ages.* It was too easy for the *wrong* type of prison officials to violate religious equality and freedom. The sweat lodge ceremony was the only ritual remaining, and the administration acted with absolute impunity over Native American religious members. Whenever a policy was fixed, things would eventually revert to the old ways. The more things changed, the more they stayed the same.

Litigation for Religious Freedom

After the passage of RFRA in 1993, advocates still urged for passage of an act to protect Native American rights. The Native American Free Exercise of Religion Act (S. 1021) was introduced to the 103rd Congress but was never passed. Chairman of the Senate Committee on Indian Affairs, Senator Inouye introduced the Native American Cultural Protection and Free Exercise of Religion Act (S. 2269) which was stalled by the Senate Energy and Natural Resources Committee.

The RFRA and RLUIPA Acts have not been able to protect Native American religious freedom in all cases. Recently, the building and use of a sweat lodge was denied in Fowler v.

Crawford, 534 F. 3d 931 (8th Cir. 2008) which the court relied on the decision in Hamilton v. Schriro, 74 F. 3d 1545 (8th Cir. 1996) where denial of a sweat lodge did not violate RFRA so therefore did not violate RLUIPA either. Ironically, it seems that case law is stronger for RLUIPA in the 9th Circuit, even though sweat lodge use may have originated from states located in the 8th Circuit.

After the passage of RFRA, prison wardens and attorney generals created a storm of backlash against prisoner litigation. The officials attempted to associate the religious freedom movement for prisoners with cases in which prisoners were filing frivolous and excessive lawsuits. A proposed amendment to exclude prisoners from RFRA protection was barely defeated by a vote of 58 – 41 in the Senate.

The prisoner anti-litigation movement silenced proposed Native American religious freedom acts. Several acts were introduced to Congress to hinder prison lawsuits. In 1996, the passage of the Prisoners Litigation Reform Act (PLRA) changed the way prisoner's lawsuits are litigated. Some of the provisions of the PLRA include:

- Preliminary injunctions are limited to 90 days

- Limitations on attorney's fees rewards

- No compensation for mental or emotional suffering

- Must pay filing fee

- Can be barred for filing frivolous or malicious lawsuits and for failure to state claim

- Any compensation received from a claim must be used to pay any restitution owed first

For federal prisoners, if a claim is malicious, harassing or includes false testimony, the prisoner can lose *good time* (early release) credits.

Inside the prison setting, litigation is usually not an option for prisoners because of the cost, issues from retaliation and general loss of faith in the legal system. Apathy has grown from years of harsh treatment and unanswered calls for help. Some Native American prisoners leave the prisons stating that they will help from the outside, but Native inmates never hear from them again. In the case of the ADOC Native inmates, they sent letters to Native groups, but many of the addresses were undeliverable. They wrote to the ACLU, but the organization didn't write back, and their families were too busy or lived too far away to help, so no one knew what to do.

The Arizona Native American circle took their grievance over the sweat lodge desecration to the top level, to the Director. The answers from prison officials for desecrating the sweat lodge stated that policy was properly followed, and nothing was done wrong.

Grey Bear drafted a lawsuit with interrogatories, summons and a brief using several sources for guidance. The case, however, in his mind lacked a good claim that would stand against the prison's inevitable assertion of security interests. The threat of further retaliation loomed over the Native American's. The court filing fee was too much money to undertake, in a case doomed to failure; they had no legal representation or the money to retain a law firm. So initially, the Native inmates decided not to file a case.

CHAPTER 2

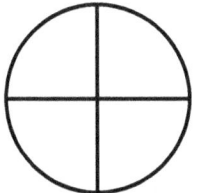

GREY BEAR SUES THE ARIZONA DEPARTMENT OF CORRECTIONS

Introduction

Litigation will never be able to fix a system that is inherently oppressive. Some say dealing with prison administration is like playing a chess game. That's not true, it's more like a boxing match and the Native American inmates keep getting punched without putting their hands up to defend themselves. For decades, Native American prisoner rights have been violated, while the prisons in America continue to incarcerate the Red Nation, thus making the prisoners like caged eagles.

Eventually, Grey Bear rallied the Native inmates. Imagine fifty upset Indians trying to decide on a solution after their sweat lodge had been desecrated. He stepped forward and yelled, "We must fill out grievance forms." Since Grey Bear had completed a grievance form in the past, he could help the other brothers complete their paperwork. The brothers got silent, as there was an unspoken code that existed concerning filing grievances. The silence was quite dramatic.

Older brothers who had been around for a long time had adhered to the unspoken rule – not to ever write kites or grievances and not to stir up trouble. In the past, filing a grievance guaranteed getting thrown in the hole. The pipe holder broke circle and ran inside. At that point the Native inmates were discussing what to include in the grievance.

Because of the proliferation of lawsuits, prisoners heard and experienced fewer *beat downs,* but prison officials still had a bag of retaliation tactics for the Native inmates; as they would find out when the pipe holder had all his electronic items taken without cause and gates were placed on the sweat lodge grounds.

The time came and went to file a lawsuit over the sweat lodge desecration. Many of the brothers had failed to follow through with the proper grievance paperwork. Grey Bear counseled some of them about the chances of winning a lawsuit. The claim would have to do with how a search could be conducted. He didn't have access to any case law without money to pay for research, so his advice was to go for it. The three-hundred-and-fifty dollar filing fee was the main deterrent for anyone following through with the required court paperwork.

It had been Grey Bear's experience that asking for permission to do the right thing is self-defeating. The only way Native American prisoners can attain their religious freedom in America is by suing for it. Fear is what lost the Native Americans their rights up to this point. So, there are times when a Native inmate must go against the votes of the circle. At the circle, two brothers announced they had filed a lawsuit over the desecration of the sweat lodge and their religious items. This was a surprise to everyone, as the Native inmates didn't think anyone would file, as it was an unwritten rule that before anyone writes kites or any other paperwork it was to be brought to the circle first.

Grey Bear Filed Grievances Against the Arizona Department of Corrections

In April 2010, Grey Bear filed grievances citing multiple issues. The grievances stated,

> "The religious rights of the Native American inmates at Central Arizona Correctional Facility have been substantially burdened at (CACF) by Geo Group, Arizona Department of Corrections, Chaplain M. de la Cruz, Sr. Chaplain Mike Linderman, Warden John Gay, Deputy Warden Bennie Rollins, and Director Dora B. Schriro (at the time of publishing, Charles L. Ryan).

> It is not fair that Native Americans are not allowed access to their religious grounds; only once a week for prayer, smudging, and religious activity while the Christians have access to religious services, programs, and classes in their chapel every day of the week."

In 904, the first paragraph on page one, gives a substantive policy statement, then the second paragraph undoes it by providing a means to create a hidden policy using memos and no-posted regulations that infringe on our religious rights. Upon review of Arizona Revised Statutes Title 41 Grey Bear realized that the substantiative policy statement, two paragraphs, were required to be in policy by law.

Grey Bear also learned that the administration could not legally make rules in policy that were onerous. So, rather than include rules that substantially burden the religious rights in policy, prison officials crafted memorandums that denied beadwork, denied religious ground access, and contrabanded the kettle drum.

He then requested a weekly talking circle from the Chaplain. After the Chaplain consulted the Senior Chaplain, it was denied. The brothers were told that they needed a volunteer present and that they could only have a talking circle in the place of a sweat ceremony by having it in the Christian multi-denominational chapel under the direct supervision of the Chaplain. No spiritual advisors were available to be present.

It was unreasonable to tell them to pray and play their instruments in the multi-denominational religious grounds. There were no direct provisions for drums, flutes or gourds in policy. They required policy to be added to protect them from discrimination.

The responses Grey Bear received were quotes from policy from the different levels of appeals. Most of the prison officials and supervisors ignored his requests, and some of the statements were misconstrued in the responses of the appeals from the greivances he filed with the prison system. The Appeals Officer who works in the director's office states,

"You are encouraged to seek possible outside sources who can provide religious items not available (gourd and corn pollen) through the Keefe corporation. Please notify the Chaplain at your unit of any possible outside sources."

Grey Bear found that the Native brothers had access to a lot more vendors for religious herbs than he previously thought. So the corn pollen issue was one he decided to take up later. Also, in the final response, "...Private prisons shall conduct activities in accordance with the contract requirements. Please note that talking circles may only be scheduled in the absence of the weekly sweat lodge ceremony."

Also, in the final response from the Pastoral Activities Administrator, "The approved religious property list permits you to possess a beaded necklace; however, it does not allow for possession of beadwork items for the purpose of hobby or craft."

Grey Bear knew one Native American in the circle possessed the prison's idea of a *beaded necklace* and knew several who, like himself, had been trying to get a traditional choker necklace for years.

The term talking circle was noted in Rose Ann Kisto's manual on Native American religious practice for the ADOC. It's an irony how administrators were trying to use the *talking circle* to force Indians into the Christian chapel.

He drafted and submitted the following grievance to clarify his intentions and requests, which were ignored in the first grievance. Grey Bear wrote:

> "Memos, rules, and other restrictions causing a substantial burden to Native American religion should be removed and rendered void. This includes restrictions on beadwork, sweat lodge access, and musical instruments and any other rule, memo, or restriction.
>
> A lack of policy for Native American rights causes a substantial burden to our Free Exercise of Religion.

> Policy regarding medicine bags, herbs, tobacco ties, the sacred pipe, the talking circle ceremony, private worship, special ceremonies, ceremonial codes of conduct, conduct on Native American religious grounds, musical instruments, beadwork, and any other important aspect of our religion must be added to religious policy in order to protect our rights. The AZDOC *Native American Religious Services Program Manual* by Rose Ann Kisto and the US Department of Justice *Inmate Religious Beliefs and Practices* should be referenced as a guide."

Grey Bear added another issue in an appeal. Since it wasn't originally stated in an informal grievance, he wasn't able to bring it up in civil court unless he started another grievance regarding the issue. He wrote,

> "There have been excessive violations of the First Amendment and 14th Amendment of the Constitution at CACF. There are 4 Christian stations on our T.V. 7 days out of the week the Christian Chapel has turnouts for the Christians. Every newsletter I've seen has had only Christian announcements from the Chaplain. I have seen only Christian announcements on the bulletin boards. This is establishment of religion by Geo and the ADOC. Every time the Native Americans have asked for help we have been covered with a blanket of denial. You have been indifferent and suppressive to Native American religion."

The responses Grey Bear received from this second grievance stated that issues one and two were already answered in the first grievance he filed. The Appeals Officer wrote,

> "Although the CCTV offers predominately Christian programming to seventy-five percent of the inmate population, the Department will accept donated videos that do not require copyright permission for showing during religious services or multi-faith gatherings. The Department is continuously seeking donations for all religions. You are also encouraged to seek for outside

sources who are willing to provide religious videos for viewing. Please notify the Chaplain at your unit of any possible outside sources."

A few *copyright, permission free* videos wouldn't equalize the one-sided cable programs.

Grey Bear followed through on the grievances and filed additional paperwork specific to the kettle drum, the requirement to prove race as a Native American and for obtaining wood.

The history of incarceration for Native American prisoners and the resulting denial of religious freedom would lead to the Native American prisoners at Grey Bears's unit to do what? It was the historical treatment of Native Americans in the United States that led to the court case Grey Bear and his Native brothers were building against the Arizona Department of Corrections. This case was not a response of revenge or hate, but of the simple desire to practice their religion. They were being restricted in a manner that went beyond what was reasonable with safety concerns for the prison administrators. Their voices were ignored. And so, they made their concerns heard in the most powerful way they could beyond bars.

CHAPTER 3

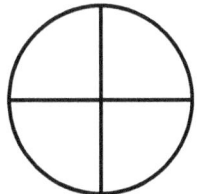

FILING THE COURT CASE

Grey Bear obtained a 1983 Civil Rights Complaint Packet from the prison library in March 2011, made a copy and started to complete it. The form is required to be filled out by the federal court system. Grey Bear read in legal magazines and books that completing the Complaint Packet was the way to seek remedy for the Native American religious practitioners if a civil right was violated. RLUIPA was the way to go.

The civil rights form for Arizona, which is in the 9th Circuit, came with instructions, but Grey Bear still consulted other prisoners who had filed lawsuits for other issues on how to complete the forms. The ADOC policy required that a paralegal be available for consultation, so Grey Bear submitted the required request and met with the paralegal twice. They did not offer any information about what to write about the case, but did help by double checking that all the required information was filled out.

Grey Bear listed himself as the Plaintiff and all the prison officials who were involved in the denials of Native American rights as the Defendants. The defendants started with the Chaplain, then the Warden, other Administrators and the Pastoral Activities Administrator who answered the grievances. Grey Bear did not ask for a jury trial because he learned that other lawsuits for inmates on similar issues were won without juries.

The prison address was listed for the plaintiff. The form asked if the plaintiff (Grey Bear) had filed any prior lawsuits. He hadn't.

The difficult part was completing the *Statement of Claims*. Grey Bear had filed many grievances on behalf of the Native American prisoners, but only those that had been sent to all of the defendants could be used in the case.

For example, the kettle drum grievance had been submitted in a timely manner to the Chaplain, the Warden, and the Pastoral Activities Administrator and all were denied; so, this complaint could be filed in federal court. Grey Bear made eight separate statement of claims and each issue had to have occurred within one year of the submission date. Each claim had its own specific relief which was completed on the next section of the form. Grey Bear submitted the required information handwritten as small as possible, so that all the claims and relief fit on the form.

He filled out all the information and had it notarized at the prison library. On May 9, 2011 Grey Bear sent the several required copies to the court and his case was filed. Several months later, the court sent him an official memorandum stating that the packet had been reviewed and Gabriel (Grey Bear) was sent another packet to complete. He needed to complete more forms so all the defendants could be served with a summons. Since a three-hundred-and-fifty dollar fee was required to file, Grey Bear learned that the fee could be paid with payments, also known as *In Forma Pauperis*. A payment was made from his paycheck every week while he worked in the prison washing dishes and cleaning the cafeteria.

Grey Bear made copies of all the inmate letters and grievances that involved the claims and submitted it to the court during the *discovery* process. Discovery is when the court asks for all the evidence of the case from both sides. Again, Grey Bear paid all the required court paperwork fees with his own money.

The court first had to decide if the case was valid, then give the plaintiffs and defendants instructions on how to proceed. The court checked to ensure that the grievances were sent to all the Defendants involved in a timely manner. Then the defendants were given a chance to respond to the Plaintiff's complaint. The judge was aware that the Plaintiff was a prisoner and did not have legal training, but gave the Plaintiff time to correct paperwork errors that were submitted to the court.

Grey Bear had to rewrite his claims in a way that was clear to the court; this time he used legal citations which he gathered from legal books in the library. He had taken the Blackstone paralegal course while incarcerated and was able to write a sufficient case to *pass summary judgement,* which means that if the allegations in the complaint were true, then the Plaintiff would have a valid case which should be remedied by the Defendant. Each submission of paperwork to the court was followed up and it took months until the court was satisfied. Then the other side had time to respond to the allegations.

Grey Bear received a positive judgement on four of the eight claims for the summary judgement. At one point he received a letter from the Perkins Coie Law Firm stating that they would like to represent him and the case *pro bono*, (without a fee). Grey Bear met with three lawyers in the prison visitation room who would represent the Native American prisoner's religious rights in this case. The three attorneys (one woman and two men) worked with Gabriel from this point forward to file the correct forms, find more discovery objects for the case, and create a pre-trial brief for the court case.

They documented all aspects of the sweat lodge and its desecration in the discovery process and took photos of the lodge area and religious chapel at the prison. They contacted the prison repeatedly to see if a settlement could be worked out before the case went to court. The settlement process did not bear fruit, so the Plaintiff, Defendants and all their lawyers met for a bench trial at the federal courthouse in Phoenix, Arizona.

There were several days of testimony. The Plaintiff and Defendants called on the ADOC Chief of Security, the Pastoral Activities Administrator, the Chaplain at the prison, and several Native American Spiritual Advisors.

For the plaintiff, Grey Bear was the first person to testify. He was shuttled several times from the Florence prison to Phoenix. Initially, it was a very stressful experience and he lost a lot of sleep over it. He prayed to the Creator to assist him and the lawyers in this case. He was allowed to return to the federal court for the opening and closing deliberations, and several months later for a procedural issue.

Leo Killsback, from the Northern Cheyenne Nation and an Assistant Professor of American Indian studies at Arizona State University testified on the religious practices of Native Americans. Lenny Foster, Director of the *Navajo Nation Corrections Project* testified regarding his experiences on building sweat lodges in Arizona and other state prisons. He also discussed how the kettle drum was allowed in federal prisons and how the kettle drum was no longer allowed in Arizona prisons. When Lenny Foster entered the courtroom, the lights in the room flashed and the court recording system shut down, causing a significant delay in the proceedings. Grey Bear felt it was the power of God that overloaded the system.

CHAPTER 4

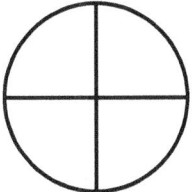

THE CLAIMS AND SETTLEMENTS

A settlement for two of the four claims was signed on February 13, 2014. These settlements allowed for the addition of the sacred water drum to the Native American religious items list and to ensure that Native Americans can have smudges outside with the talking circle. See Sharp v. Geo Group Inc., et al., cv11-00925PHX-R05.

The Water Drum Claim and Settlement

The kettle drum claim enabled the Plaintiff to point out to the court that the inmates lived on metal bunks and that a metal flute was allowed in the chapel for the music program. Making these points was important because the Defendants wanted to deny use of a kettle drum because it was made of metal. To this point, and the fact that kettle drums were allowed in the past in the Arizona prisons, the Pastoral Activities Administrator agreed to a settlement allowing the Native American prisoners to have a kettle drum for religious practice.

The Talking Circle Claim and Settlement

The talking circle claim led to the admission by the Pastoral Activities Administrator that talking circles were permitted outside so the Native American prisoners could smudge. The Pastoral Activities Administrator agreed to settle the issue about talking circles being allowed outdoors for smudging with a written settlement agreed to and signed by both sides.

The Sweat Lodge Firewood Claim and Settlement

In court, the Plaintiff's lawyers discussed with the Pastoral Activities Administrator, the head of security operations, and the unit chaplain the issues that were involved in having firewood delivered to Native American inmates. The testimonies and evidence showed that sweat ceremonies at that prison unit were sometimes delayed for months because of the few donations of firewood that the inmates would receive. The existing process only allowed for firewood to be brought into the prison by an outsider and only once the request was approved. The Native inmates requested the ability to purchase their own firewood with their own money and with community donations. The Defendants refused to allow the proposed process; therefore, they refused to settle this claim.

Several months passed before a verdict in favor of Gabriel Sharp, the Plaintiff, on behalf of his Native American brothers for the sweat lodge firewood was issued. On September 29, 2014 an Amended Final Judgement granted the RLUIPA claim for the Plaintiff, allowing a path for Native American prisoners in Arizona to purchase their own firewood for sweat ceremonies. This judgement enabled Native inmates to pool their money together and allowed for community members to donate funds in order to purchase firewood. Inmate funds and donations would be processed through the prison chaplain. Initially the judgement allowed for a group account for the Native Americans; but the Defendants asked for an amended judgement.

The Defendants lost. They wanted an agreement with the Native inmates as to what was required of them because ADOC didn't want to have to provide group accounts for all the religious groups. An agreement was negotiated between the Native American prisoners and the ADOC on ways for the Native Americans to obtain firewood for the sweat lodge ceremony. The amended agreement gave the Native American prisoners the ability to obtain sweat lodge firewood, and it was now a legal judgement.

The settlements were negotiated between both sides, then signed. Then the amended agreement was negotiated and signed in the same manner. The negotiations took several months as the agreements were sent back and forth between the parties. The entire case would take three years from start to finish.

UNITED STATES DISTRICT COURT
DISTRICT OF ARIZONA

Gabriel Sheridan Sharp Plaintiff vs. Geo Group, et al., Defendants	No. CV 11-00925-PHX-ROS (DKD) **AMENDED FINAL JUDGMENT**

The Amended Final Judgment now reads:

Native American Indian ("NAI") inmates incarcerated with the Arizona Department of Corrections ("ADC") (whether in public or private facilities) who are authorized pursuant to ADC policy to participate in sweat lodge ceremonies may purchase firewood to be used exclusively for the purpose of sweating in a sweat lodge, subject to the following conditions:

a. Application: All individual and group requests to purchase sweat lodge ceremony firewood shall be submitted, by way of an inmate letter, to the complex chaplain;

b. Source: Firewood must be purchased through an ADC approved source and delivered through ADC approved channels;

c. Individual Sweat: If any NAI inmate desires to purchase firewood for an individual sweat, the inmate must make this preference known to the complex chaplain when he or she first applies for a firewood purchase. No other inmates will be allowed to contribute to the firewood purchase or participate in the individual sweat;

d. Commodification: NAI inmates shall not trade, loan, barter or sell any firewood to staff, a visitor, contractor, volunteer, or another inmate, consistent with DO 909.02.1.2;

e. <u>Group Sweat</u>: A group of NAI inmates may decide to make a group purchase of firewood. NAI inmates who wish to contribute to the purchase of firewood for a group sweat lodge ceremony shall advise the complex chaplain of their intent, by way of an inmate letter indicating the amount each inmate will contribute towards the total purchase price of the specified quantity of firewood. Each contributing inmate will release funds from their inmate trust accounts (ITAs) pursuant to DO 905.03.1.1.2.12. Inmate banking will submit the firewood order to the approved source along with the total amount of funds for the purchase and delivery of the order of firewood to the complex. The group purchase request shall be denied if total funds from individual inmates contributing to the group purchase is insufficient to cover the total price, including taxes and delivery charges, of the specified order, and inmates will need to submit a new request;
f. <u>Approved Source</u>: An approved source is a legitimate wholesale or retail outlet verified by ADC's Administrator of Pastoral Activities or a designee, that agrees to sell and arrange for delivery of approved religious items and materials to inmates;
g. <u>Non-Selectivity</u>: If any NAI inmate purchases or contributes to the purchase of firewood for a group sweat lodge ceremony, the sweat will be open to any and all inmates in his/her unit who are eligible to participate in sweat lodge ceremonies. Group sweat lodge ceremonies will be conducted consistent with DO 904;
h. <u>Donations</u>: Members of the community (individuals, tribes, approved groups, and approved companies) may donate sweat lodge firewood to ADC families for sweat lodge use;
i. <u>Purchases</u>: Members of the community (individuals, tribes, approved groups, and approved companies) may purchase sweat lodge firewood for use by NAI inmates at ADC facilities for sweat lodge use. Members of the community may donate funds through the complex chaplain to contribute to group purchases of firewood pursuant to Paragraph (e) above by submitting an ADC Offer of Gift/Donation Form, Form 301-1, to the ADC and indicating that the purpose of the donation is restricted to the purpose of group purchase of firewood for sweat ceremonies;

j. <u>Prohibition Against Individual Leverage</u>: Members of the community may not donate firewood to individual inmates, but may send money to a specific inmate, who can then elect to purchase firewood for an individual or group sweat lodge ceremony;

k. <u>Caveat Emptor</u>: ADC and its staff are not liable for any firewood that is damaged, destroyed, or otherwise rendered unusable in delivery or in storage, except as provided for in DO 909. Purchasing inmates are responsible for using any sweat lodge firewood in a timely manner. Any property claims for negligent or intentional destruction of firewood by ADC shall be governed by DO 909.09;

l. <u>Release From Custody</u>: Upon release, NAI inmate firewood purchasers shall make arrangements to donate or otherwise dispose of the firewood consistent with DO 909.02.1.2;

m. <u>DO 904</u>: Defendants shall immediately integrate the terms of this Order into DO 904.

IT IS SO ORDERED.

s/ Jack Zouhary
JACK ZOUHARY
U. S. DISTRICT JUDGE

September 29, 2014

SETTLEMENT AGREEMENT

Plaintiff Gabriel Sheridan Sharp and Defendants Arizona Department of Corrections ("ADC") Director Charles Ryan and ADC Administrator of Pastoral Activities Michael Linderman, and John Gay as Warden at Central Arizona Correctional Facility (collectively "the Parties"), hereby agree to dismiss portions of their lawsuit—11-cv-00925-PHX (the "lawsuit")—with prejudice. The following recitations reflect the understanding of the Parties:

1. The Parties agree that a kettle drum (also known as a water drum), described below, is hereby added to the approved religious materials and supplies list;

2. Kettle drums are identified as round drums, constructed of metal, wood, pottery, or gourds, with a detachable leather skin covering the opening. Seven to twenty marble-sized rocks are placed in the drum before adding water and attaching the covering. The hide is secured to the drum with string or twine;

3. Kettle drums designated for Native American Religious ("NAR") group use must be donated to the ADC and Arizona private prisons, including GEO Group's facilities, consistent with ADC religious donation policy;

4. Donated kettle drums will be available for use by members of the NAR group during group ceremony or worship in Talking Circles or any other NAR group turnouts. Metal kettle drums are permitted for use in sweat lodge areas (not inside the sweat lodge), in line of site of correctional officers;

5. This Settlement Agreement extinguishes any and all claims included in the lawsuit against Defendants Charles Ryan, Michael Linderman, and John Gay related to or arising out of kettle drums and water drums with prejudice;

6. The Parties further agree that NAR group Talking Circles must be held outdoors when the group chooses to smudge;

7. The Parties agree that Michael Linderman will e-mail a reminder memorandum to chaplains at Central Arizona Correctional Facility and all private Arizona state prisons indicating:

> Chaplains,
>
> As you are no doubt aware, Talking Circles are often held in conjunction with the Multi-Faith Gathering turnout on the weeks when no Sweat occurs or when a Native American volunteer is available to lead them. There has been some confusion about Talking Circles at one of the private prisons and therefore this is just a reminder that Native American Talking Circles are ceremonies that involve smudging (smoke

generating activity). As such, Talking Circles are permitted outdoors so that participants may smudge. It is not appropriate to restrict Talking Circles to inside a building unless on a one-time basis for a specific security or operational concern.

A copy of this memorandum must be posted in the Chaplain's office for a period of 30 days upon receipt.

8. Defendants, through counsel, will provide Sharp's counsel with a copy of the transmission, as well as proof of its transmission;

9. This Settlement Agreement extinguishes any and all claims included in the lawsuit against Defendants Charles Ryan and Michael Linderman related to or arising out of Talking Circles being held outdoors;

10. The Parties agree to immediately execute and file a Stipulation to Dismiss these portions of the lawsuit;

11. The Parties agree that the remaining claims and issues in the lawsuit remain outstanding and are unaffected by this Settlement Agreement;

12. This Settlement Agreement is not an admission of liability by Defendants;

13. This Settlement Agreement represents the entire agreement of the Parties regarding these claims; and

14. This Settlement Agreement is to be construed consistent with the laws of the State of Arizona.

Executed this 13 Day of February, 2014

Sambo Dul
Bridget Minder
Daniel Barr
Attorneys for Plaintiff Gabriel Sharp

Executed this ___ Day of February, 2014

Pari Scroggin
Attorney for Warden Gay

Executed this 13th Day of February, 2014

Michael Hrnicek
Office of the Attorney General of Arizona
Attorney for Defendants Ryan and Linderman

CHAPTER 5

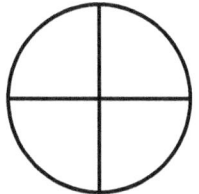

ACTIONS AFTER THE LAWSUIT

With assistance from the unit Chaplain, Grey Bear helped to establish a firewood vendor that would deliver firewood for the sweat lodge at the prison where he was incarcerated; the Pastoral Activities Administrator received and approved the request. The Native American inmates submitted inmate letters and forms to the unit chaplain requesting a group purchase of firewood and how much they each wanted to donate. They immediately pooled their funds and family members sent money to the approved vendor in order to purchase firewood for the sweat lodge ceremonies and had it delivered to the prison. In early 2015, the Native American inmates were holding sweat lodge ceremonies by gaining wood through the agreed upon process, a method that was never allowed previously.

The lawyers from the Perkins Coie Law Firm donated the brand-new kettle drum that was used in discovery for the court case to the Native American prisoners. This was the first kettle drum officially allowed in the Arizona Department of Corrections. It was kept safe in a locked closet in the multi-faith room (chapel) at the prison and allowed for use during Native American ceremonies.

The prison chaplains would summon Grey Bear and ask for guidance regarding any issues concerning Native American religious practice. The guards and inmates at the prison learned about the lawsuit and treated him with respect. Inmates occasionally consulted Grey Bear with advice on grievances and lawsuits. Prison guards and officials treated him as an equal during any interaction and he didn't experience any conflicts with prison officials after the case.

Grey Bear continued to attend Native American ceremonies every week. He was the main Native American singer at his prison and started a drum group and became the drum carrier, the person who took care of the drum and gourds. The drum group sang at the yearly Pow Wows that the Native American religious group held at the prison with outside guests.

At some point, Grey Bear was criticized by other Native American prisoners during the court case and afterward for filing the paperwork. Because of jealousy and prison politics, Grey Bear was replaced as the drum carrier, but he still sang and attended every ceremony despite his critics. Eventually, his critics were moved to other prisons through regular inmate rotations. Before he finished his sentence, Grey Bear founded the *Pow Wow Committee* at the prison along with four other Native American inmates, who planned the yearly Pow Wow and gathered funds for the sweat ceremony.

At the beginning of 2017, a new Pastoral Activities Administrator for the Arizona Department of Corrections was hired. The process to gain firewood still allowed for the same provisions that were won in the case. Policy also gave the chaplain the authority to determine along with the warden, the number of religious activities that the inmates require. Also, according to policy, all smoke generating ceremonies must be conducted outside. The changes that were made in policy because of this court case, continue to this day. Steps need to be taken to create a dialogue between Native American prisoners and people on the outside so ADOC policy doesn't revert to old ways.

In 2017, Grey Bear was released from prison and began a new life.

GREY BEAR STANDS UP

Prison officials lack the knowledge to understand the religious beliefs of Native Americans. Even more so, they prefer to remain aloof because knowledge equals responsibility. Why is it the Native Americans must litigate for religious freedom? Why are Native American religious groups in prisons so oppressed?

Without litigation, the Native American religious groups would hardly exist. In truth, Native American prisoners will rarely litigate, for fear of reprisal. For each known story of Native American religious intolerance, how many unknown situations are happening nationwide daily?

There are two major reasons the Native American prisoners won't file grievances or litigate when their rights are being violated. First, administration and other officials overseeing the religious group had and would retaliate against the group if one complained or asked for anything. For example, when the brothers requested an additional drum for the group, the Chaplain took away the existing kettle drum that had been used for years. It took almost an entire year to get a replacement drum and the requested additional drum never came to fruition; and on several occasions, the administration threatened to reduce the time allotted for the service when they asked for something, like equal treatment.

Second, it costs time and money to file a case against the system. Three hundred and fifty dollars to file documents for a court case is a lot of money to anyone who is incarcerated. The highest paying job is forty-five cents an hour, and those positions are limited. Most inmates are afraid to write a kite to file a grievance or don't know how to file a court case; nor would an inmate ever want to, given the retaliation guaranteed by officers which could be in the form of harassment or getting shipped to the next unit.

We need help getting lava rocks, willow poles and wood for our sweat ceremonies, so that we can conduct talking circles and organize Pow Wows. We need members of the Native American Church (NAC) to teach us NAC songs. We need practitioners of the Sun Dance Way help us with the inipi and sacred pipe. We need guidance to help find the Corn Pollen Road and the Red Road toward redemption and enlightenment.

In order to keep track of repression from prison officials toward our group, I kept a timeline of events and summarized each issue that arose. I kept several journals and wrote reports to help describe events to people on the outside. Many of the reports ended up in the *Native American Prisoners Journals* that we wrote and mailed to different newspapers and advocates. Over the course of these writings, prison officials found different ways to hinder our group, one being that family members could not order spiritual items or herbs from the outside. Another was the required process for Native American inmates to obtain spiritual items. The paperwork, money needed and length of time to receive herbs, which could take up to three months were all deterrents.

We need help from people on the outside to create positive change for Native American prisoners in Arizona. We need to *Stand Up* so that we can have the traditional feast allowed for the Pow Wow ceremony. We need to *Stand Up* so that we can obtain all the required items for our religious practice. We need to *Stand Up* so that we can have talking circles and pipe ceremonies allowed at our sacred sweat lodge grounds.

Come on brothers and sisters! *Stand Up for Your People!*

SOLUTIONS

Dear Walks in Faith,

Change only comes with great struggle. You were born a great shepherd. The empathy and understanding you have is a great gift. You will walk through the shadows and valleys, through the foothills to save your flock. But the sheep will only walk to where the grass grows green, where they can find comfort in their sleep. Like a good shepherd, you rest little, wary of the night.

But it's time to wake up brother. It's time to wake up from this dream we created for ourselves. It's time to speak out and do the right thing despite the adversity we face. It's time to leave the sheep behind and soar with the eagles. We must stand up as men and become who we are called to be. Those who wish to stand, will follow; those who don't, will find their own way. We must soar where the Creator meant for us to be.

Is it not the lowest, cruelest and most degrading form of discrimination for the penological system to deny our Red brothers and sisters their First Amendment right of religious freedom? Why have the administrators and directors at the prison and ADOC not stepped in to stop the systematic oppression of incarcerated Native Americans? Does no one within this system have the moral insight to consider the mental and emotional trauma they are causing our people?

We must stand not just for our own rights, but for our brothers and sisters at other units as well. If officers can violate our beliefs in our unit, then it has happened at other units and throughout the State of Arizona. How many other sweat lodges throughout the United States have been desecrated?

If the cost of freedom is the loss of some privileges that our brothers at the next unit don't have, then why should we have them? Our circles are one, we shouldn't benefit while others suffer. If the chaplain told me the price of religious freedom was my gourd, then they can keep it. I will not let them dangle freedom in front of me like a carrot. I am not going to let them control my direction.

Well brother, it looks like there are some serious issues that must be faced. That is all I have to say.

Grey Bear
Mitakuye Oyasin

CHAPTER 1

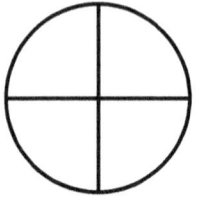

INTRODUCTION

It is important to set a goal and take steps to achieve it. Sometimes after action is taken, you may find yourself even farther from the goal than before. Never stop or slow down. Failure can only be a lesson; pick yourself up, dust yourself off and jump back in.

The greatest leaders are the ones who took risks, missed and recovered. You can become good at something even if you have become weathered to the despairing sting of failure. You can become great at something when adversity strikes you head on, but you need to keep moving forward. Always keep in mind that things may get worse before they get any better.

Martin Luther King Jr. was jailed for non-violent protests that he took part in on April 16th, 1963, in Birmingham, Alabama. During the protests, police blasted the protesters with water from fire hoses and released police dogs on them. Many of the protesters were women and children. Photographs were taken and seen around the world. President Kennedy intervened regarding the issues and eventually equal rights were achieved.

There are few ways to solve policy issues in prison. Native American prisoners, their families and community members need to be vigilant about supporting Native American prisoner's rehabilitation. To keep Native American spiritual oppression from repeating, events that occur need to be documented. Also, an organization needs to be created that supports incarcerated Native American prisoners and their families. The *Native*

American Prisoners Support Network is an idea for a non-profit agency that Grey Bear would like to start to support Native Americans in prisons. Native American prisoners need to write about the things that are happening in prison and communicate it.

The action Grey Bear suggests is a written campaign, as only prison officials benefit from any kind of physical protests. When inmates riot or attack guards, it is a result of inmates feeling like their rights are being violated and the only way to correct the wrong is through physical violence against the prison guards and by destroying the prison. If the Native American religious practitioners riot because they feel their rights are violated, then prison officials call in the riot squad to deal with the prisoners. Both prisoners and guards are injured.

Prison officials will then send the Native American prisoners and their leadership who were involved in the riot to the segregation unit. After spending time in segregation, the Native inmates are usually sent to different prisons. This effectively resets the Native American population in a unit and becomes a repetitive process of desecration and violence. Although some physical actions may seem like a loss in the beginning, it can be worth the knowledge and perseverance that is gained.

CHAPTER 2

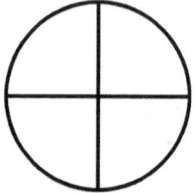

WRITTEN COMMUNICATION

Formal Written Policy

Code of Conduct Policy: A policy needs to be written to protect and define *sacred* objects and *appropriate respect* related to officer and staff behavior toward Native Americans and their ceremonial items.

Standard of Ethics: A reference needs to be set as a foundation of Native American beliefs. The *standard* should be based on Native American spiritual practices and provide a basis for how prison officials can interact with Native American religious practitioners in a way that prevents conflict. Some entries in the standard should include how sacred items should be handled by prison guards and how to search the sweat lodge without desecrating it. Manuals and prison policies can be researched for the best language to be used so that the simultaneous needs of both Native American religious practitioners and prison officials are met.

The main cause of conflict now, as well as throughout history, is a misunderstanding of each other's needs and finding a compromise to fulfill those needs. A reasonable policy for Native American spiritual beliefs needs to be written to include the definition of *sacred* and what is considered *appropriate* behavior in and around sacred areas. Otherwise, any person who works for the Department of Corrections can interpret or twist the definitions to fit their own needs or circumstances. There have been provisions written in the past on how searches should be conducted without conflict. Policy has been removed and changed in ways that have resulted in the desecration of the Native inmate's sacred items. History repeats itself. The refusal of administration to correct policy and admit to no wrongdoing is a substantial burden on the Native Americans Free Exercise of Religion. All these issues have been brought up repeatedly in the US Court System.

If a situation isn't solved through a verbal conversation, then there are two options: 1) let it go, or 2) file paperwork.

Let a situation go and one's rights continue to be violated by the system. It is inevitable that history will repeat itself and most likely become worse. Filing paperwork as a grievance requires follow through and this may mean filing a civil action in court.

Unfortunately, Native Americans have become so accustomed to being oppressed that no one has stepped forward to change the outcome of religious rights. It is up to Native Americans to challenge and change the system themselves.

Writing to the Prison Officials

In Arizona prisons, it's against policy for inmates to help other inmates with legal work. This is a policy that is constantly broken, as the inmates view the policy as completely inhumane.

In order to follow through with the grievance system the prisoner must fill out and submit a series of paperwork. As mentioned previously, an inmate is supposed to work out a problem with the official or officer with whom they are having a conflict. Or, write an official, factual inmate letter detailing the situation; devoid of emotion or exaggeration, and providing a reasonable solution.

An inmate letter is an informal grievance written to the CPO III Counselor, a security officer of higher rank, whose job it is to settle an inmate's problems and resolve grievances at the base level. The counselor contacts the officer who the complaint is against and tries to find a resolution or justify the officer's action with policy. It is never a very happy experience.

Officers despise grievances; and inmates who write them might have an invisible target on his back. After the initial contact, the CPO III calls the inmate to their office to let him know the response to the informal grievance, and whether or not there was a solution. If not, then the inmate can elevate the complaint to the next level by filling out a different grievance form within five days of the initial of the writing. A grievance coordinator reviews the paperwork, tries to find a line in policy that justifies the officer's behavior, and writes a response.

Usually the response will summarize (sometimes inaccurately) the main idea of the grievance, quote policy that sides with the officer, and will sometimes find fault with the inmate writing the grievance. The process is then repeated by the inmate filling out a grievance appeal form, submitting it to a grievance appeal coordinator, then follows the same process and submits it to the Warden and Director who often don't view the paperwork themselves, but is reviewed by a staff person. By the time a grievance runs its course through the *kangaroo court*, the prison officials have quoted policy like it's some kind of religion for the administrators.

When writing a grievance, one needs to weigh the potential response to the action, as it may cause retaliation from either other inmates or prison staff. With staff, it usually starts with excessive searches and finding ways that allow them to state that the inmate is breaking the rules.

By the time the grievance has reached the end of the grievance process, it's possible the inmate will find him/herself on a bus to the next unit. So, inmates pick and choose their battles wisely.

Knowing the potential consequences to the grievance, follow the suggested process below:

Document, document, document – keep track of all issues in writing. This includes providing the incident that occurred (action and reaction), the date, time and witnesses. Every time an event occurs that is controversial to the Native American prisoners, the event should be written down in a journal. Copies of any inmate letters, grievances, or any other writings should be saved. Two copies should be kept in two separate files. Ask a trusted inmate to preserve one copy, while the initiator should keep the other copy. Keep a timeline of events and summarize each issue that presents itself.

Write the grievance in a respectful manner. When a grievance is written, it should be as factual as possible. Emotions and assumptions are not helpful if they are written into the context of the grievance. Three facts should be presented: what happened, why the situation is a violation, and what relief is required. Be sure to include a list of everything that happened and any witnesses to the event. Ask for help and seek out others to whom you can talk. Every now and then a staff person can be helpful.

Warning: Be careful of the words spoken and actions taken, the walls have ears, as there is no such thing as privacy in prison.

Write an Action Plan

Martin Luther King, Jr., in his letter written from a Birmingham jail, identified four important steps to take in any nonviolent campaign for freedom and equal rights. First, collect the facts and data of an adverse situation. Second, engage in communication and negotiation with the affected parties. Third, engage in preparation and self-purification. Fourth, engage in direct action.

Step One. Get the facts. How widespread are the issues and how deep is the problem(s). Determine what action has been taken to deal with the issues in the past. Who has been involved and what history exists regarding the issue. Write inmate letters asking for information and answers to specific questions. Talking face to face with officials involved is often of no value unless there are written facts confirming the issue or problem. There may be officials who will try to help, but they may face the deterrence from the administration that an inmate encounters.

Try to gain more information than is given. Keep a journal and write memos, including important dates, times and names of officials involved. Once the situation and all the components of it can be accurately assessed, move on to the next step.

Step Two. Negotiate. Negotiation involves communicating a problem, by placing both parties' issues on the table and finding a solution. At this point, the *pot* is not being stirred, but the lights of the truth are being turned on. No matter what, keep moving forward. Action changes things; do not get stuck waiting for something to happen.

Always be respectful and ask specific questions. Negotiation may lead to false promises, dead ends or outright denial. Things may get fixed one day, but may revert to the *old way* the next day. A valuable part of this step is gathering additional paperwork. Be sure to sort and organize every kite and memo.

Step Three. Self-purification. Come to terms with yourself as an inmate – who you are, what you are trying to accomplish, and how to do it. This is a very important, because inmates are only cattle to the system. Do the cattle (inmates) ever argue with the rancher (Warden)? No, so it is, an inmate must resolve oneself to communicate with the outside world. A relationship must be built with the *ranch owner,* not from the *cattle,* but from the outside world (inmate advocate).

Step Four. Written action. This final step requires other actions to take place for the plan to have a positive impact.

> • Identify the people who can help draft the written grievance. A well-written action plan takes time and the more time spent writing and re-writing, the better the proposal will become.

> • Identify and gather the facts as it relates to the situation. Talk to everyone who saw the event occur and write down the comments, as to what happened. Write down the location, time and date.

> • Create a strategy to spread the word about the action plan. Write to the tribal newspaper and find a journalist to use as a resource. Tell family members about the cause and enlist their help. The writing campaign may eventually provide benefits that cannot be predicted. People may be working in the background to aid with

the plan's execution. Save all responses and place them in a central folder. Write and send an article to tribal newspapers as some of the writings submitted may become published. Native American journalists like to hear from Native American prisoners. Write to them and if they respond consider them a contact. Send them copies of grievances and any reports or journal entries of conflicts that may occur. Some of Grey Bear's writings have appeared in the editorial section of tribal newspapers.

• Write the plan and mail it to appropriate supporters. Send the plan to those who can make copies and send it to others who may be interested in the cause. Ask other Native Americans if they have any addresses of Native American advocates, organizations and Indian centers. Draft a master letter that contains information about the cause and send it to the contacts that have been made. Use the master letter and edit it according to who is being contacted and the desired result. Don't be discouraged if only a few responses are received. Keep writing and if someone doesn't reply to the letter, keep their name on the list and send updates accordingly.

The above actions are best way to start the process of change for Native American prisoners. It takes a lot of time and effort to create change while incarcerated. Often times there will be unforeseen difficulties in the process, but what has been written and shared can be the necessary spark to light the fire needed to change things for the better. Change while incarcerated can only happen with a pen and the hand to use it. Consequently, a closed fist, violence, only leads to further suffering when prison officials react to physical threats. Taking the right steps, by using nonviolence, is the only path to freedom and redemption.

CHAPTER 3

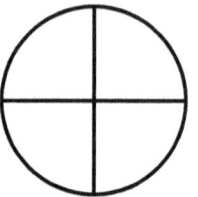

OTHER SOLUTIONS

Mediation

Mediation is one solution in which prison staff sit down with the Native inmates as equal human beings and work out an agreement to ensure the religious rights of Native Americans now and in the future. Only with education and open dialogue may future conflict be prevented.

The best way to ask for mediation is by submitting an inmate letter. Ask for a simple solution and provide a reasonable alternative. If no solution presents itself consider writing a grievance. If there are multiple issues involving a single theme, such as religious rights, address all the issues at the same time.

Sensitivity Training

Most inmates will agree that prison officers and staff need to complete religious sensitivity training. Grey Deer shared with the Native inmates that the prisons used to conduct a weekly class for officers that addressed Native American beliefs.

Training needs to be provided to the chaplain and prison staff to educate them on the sacredness of Native American tradition, culture and religion. The US Bureau of Prison developed a handbook titled, *American Indian Spirituality Beliefs and Practices* that needs to be made available and used by staff.

Grey Bear believes that a Native American or a specific officer(s) who is trained and truly respects the Native American beliefs, faith, and all that is held sacred should be the person(s) to search the sweat lodge area, sweat lodge, altar, fire pit and artifacts.

Educational Opportunities

It is important that Native American prisoners educate themselves about traditional Native American customs and values in order to prevent recidivism. Many Native Americans come into the prison system unknowledgeable of their traditions, history and indigenous language. Without this connection to their culture, they do not develop the skills to change their opportunities in life.

A resource guide written by former Native American prisoner, Frederick Fisher, inspired Grey Bear to ask the chaplain for access to use a classroom for educating Native Americans in artwork and Indian culture. He wanted to use the skills he has as a Native American artist to teach the brothers on the yard about their culture and art.

In March 2010 Grey Bear submitted an inmate letter to the Chaplain stating,

> "I would like to know if there is a way I can set up a Native American Art & Language class. The purpose would be to teach Navajo language, native history, and basic drawing skills. If we could use any of the classrooms that would be ideal. Any evening or on Sunday would be good. Ideally, I would like this program to be available to both Native and non-native alike."

The Chaplain wrote back on the kite,

> "This is something you have to organize – give me the names of those interested and ADC #'s – come see me tomorrow."

Grey Bear generated a sign-up sheet and took it to the next talking circle. Originally, he wanted the class to be open to non-natives as well, but the brothers preferred it to be a Native only class. He didn't see a problem with this since the Christian groups had more than six regular turnouts, six *Worship Team* music group turnouts, and at the time, one Hebrew/Greek class all solely for the Christians. He was also seeking approval for a talking circle.

The Native American circle looked forward to having additional opportunities together. Grey Bear wrote to the Chaplain,

> "I have tried on several occasions to get an appointment with your office, however, you were busy. I have started to gather lists on a talking circle and an art/culture class and will have all the signatures by Saturday, when I will drop them off. Wednesday evening is the preferred time for the talking circle, as many of us work or go to school. Anytime on Sunday would probably be best for the art class. So far, there has been a lot of support. I will keep the lists updated and accurate."

Grey Bear had twenty inmates signed-up for the culture class and gave the names to the Chaplain. Later that month, he received an ADOC inmate letter response from the Chaplain,

> "Your request to have a basic drawing and portrait class with periodic presentations was denied by the Deputy Warden at this time."

The brothers in the circle were extremely disappointed. Grey Bear was never given a reason for the denial of the art class and the reason for the denial of the talking circle was because of the *hidden lock out* policy.

Help from Outside – Advocates

Over two-hundred and fifty thousand Native Americans representing twenty-one federally recognized tribes live in Arizona. More support is needed for the dozens of tribal members who join the *Circle* (in prison) every year. They are the lost and forgotten members of their tribes. Advocates and family members in every state need to help create prisoner support groups for Native American prisoners. A spiritual connection needs to be made with the outside, a connection to society. This can be achieved with a spiritual advisor, but being one to a prison can become costly.

Provisions and financial compensation need to be made for an outside spiritual advisor to attend religious ceremonies. Spiritual advisors need assistance in paying for transportation and for materials such as sage, cedar and tobacco that are used in ceremonies. Also, spiritual advisors may be able to provide the Native inmates with the donation of a musical instrument or firewood for sweat ceremonies, which can help the brothers with their religious practices.

Few people know of the oppressive treatment towards Native American religious practitioners in Arizona. The difficulties and denials they have experienced shows how vulnerable the Native inmates were without adequate rules to protect Native American religious freedom in Arizona. Every state with Native American prisoners needs to have some type of support group.

For example, in South Dakota, a grass root prisoner's support group was created to help protect the rights of the Native American prisoners. Native Americans in South Dakota faced racial injustice, medical neglect and illegal conditions in prisons and jails.

Becoming an advocate for Native American spiritual rights comes with a degree of disappointment and frustration. Expect push back, even if freedom is achieved, there is always a bigger fight around the corner.

Zines

The Native American Rights Fund sent Grey Bear a copy of the *Study of Native American Prisoners Issues,* dated 1996. It was like finding a gold mine and he used the manifest as a basis for a book project that he believed would land him a *trip to the hole* and the next unit. Grey Bear decided to write a newsletter that focused on Native American issues.

A book to prisoner's program sent Grey Bear a resource called the *Prisoners Activist Resource Center Guide.* Inside the resource was the address for the South Chicago ABC Zine Distributor run by Anthony Rayson, who publishes a catalog of *zines* (magazines). He wrote Mr. Rayson and requested some zines from the catalog and received a collection of writings that went against the system, many of them written by prisoners. Half of the zines Grey Bear ordered were confiscated by the property department for a few weeks, but later delivered to him after further review. The zine themes were focused on injustice and oppression in America and many promoted the *Anarchist* movement.

One Native American zine in the catalog titled, *The Red Heart Warrior* by Tom Big Warrior was of special interest, so Grey Bear sent an inmate check for all the issues. He also received a zine crafted by a former Native American inmate and teacher, Frederick Fisher. This zine led to the idea of Grey Bear crafting his own zine. He kept a journal and wrote reports to help describe events to people on the outside; and many of his writings became part of the zine.

He ran into some roadblocks as he got started. His family was too busy help him, so he had to handwrite his own zine. Titled, the *Native American Prisoners Journal,* Grey Bear focused on the inner workings of a manipulative prison system. With knowledge gathered from other Natives, library books and experiences he was able to publish the zine every three months.

Grey Bear sent handwritten copies of the manifest to different advocacy organizations and he regularly sent the *Native American Prisoners Journal* to zine publishers. He took an English 101 class through a scholarship program provided by a local community college and through the class learned skills that helped his writing. Grey Bear sent the essay *Environmental Injustice, the Exploitation of Mother Earth* that he wrote about uranium mining on the Navajo reservation to Anthony Rayson and the Shenandoah Newspaper, and both published it.

Everything was done through small channels, rather than large public ones. The only people who knew of the *Native American Prisoner's Journal* were the publishers and some social justice organizations. Grey Bear tried to keep his zine a secret, but as time went on, a door opened, and he sent and received publications to zine publishers, who then sent copies to other prisoners. Some of the articles in the zines are included as a part of *Stand Up for Your People*.

CHAPTER 4

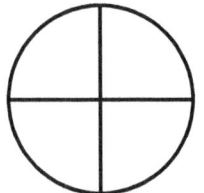

GREY BEAR'S SOLUTION

Native American Prisoners and Families Support Group

After Grey Bear's release, he had the idea to create the *Native American Prisoners and Families Support Group* (NAPRF). The Core Values, Vision and Mission statements are below.

I. Core Values Statement

>**Integrity:** Firm adherence to a code of moral values.
>
>**Cultural Identity:** The set of shared beliefs, values, goals and practices that are characteristic of the Native American community.
>
>**Resilience:** The ability to recover from or adjust to struggle or change.
>
>**Self-determination:** Free choice of one's own acts or state of being without external compulsion and determination of a people for their own status.

II. Vision Statement

>NAPRF envisions rehabilitating and educating Native American prisoners by providing resources for spiritual growth and a connection to the Native American community.

III. Mission Statement:

>The mission of NAPRF is to help provide religious items to Native American prisoners, enhance communication

between Native American prisoners and Tribal Nations, and to create and maintain a network of Native American spiritual advisors to provide religious services that promote Native American traditions.

It is Grey Bear's hope that the Native American community will join together in order to accomplish his vision. As part of the agency that Grey Bear envisions, he hopes to create and develop the following departments in order to serve Native Americans.

Religious Items Department

The goal of the Religious Items Department is to help Native American prisoners obtain religious items necessary for their religious exercise. This department also assists families in donating religious items and money to purchase religious items. Native American prisoners need help obtaining herbs for smudging, religious items for ceremonies and Native American musical instruments.

This department would keep track of all requests for religious items from Native American prisoners and their families and would be responsible for completing the necessary paperwork required for the prisoners. Spiritual advisors who visit Native American prisoners can make requests to this department.

Communication Department

The goal of the Communication Department will be to share information between tribal nations, spiritual advisors and Native American prisoners. A database of information relating to Native American resources would be maintained and shared by this department. Also, a newsletter would be sent to Native American prisoners via snail mail, while an email would be sent to supporters. Tribal members, representatives, organizations, spiritual advisors and scholars would be invited to write articles for the newsletter and would track prison events like Pow Wows and changes in policy. Also, a webpage would be maintained by this department.

Education Department

The goal of the Education Department will be to provide Native

American themed books, CDs and other instructional materials to Native American prisoners. The materials provided would give Native American prisoners references to traditional Native American values. The Education Department would also create and disseminate handbooks and printouts that would educate Native American prisoners about the Native American religion.

Religious Advisor Department

The goal of the Religious Advisor Department will be to help connect Native American prisoners with religious advisors for spiritual guidance and to assist with ceremonies. This department would actively seek out Native American spiritual advisors and would keep a list of them and the units where they can assist. Spiritual advisors would be provided with religious items so they can assist with ceremonies and those who travel long distances could request funds to pay for their expenses. This department would also seek to provide tribal members with resources so they can train to be spiritual advisors.

Fundraising Department

The goal of the Fundraising Department will be to gather funds or generate donations in order to increase revenues and assets for the organization. Donations would be obtained from different sources and would be used to implement and maintain services provided to Native American prisoners, their families and spiritual advisors. Some of the organization's fundraising activities include applying for grants, coordinating special events, conducting food fundraisers, and producing and selling Native American artwork, to name some ideas.

GREY BEAR STANDS UP

"We are human, despite the way they treat us."
Grey Bear

The Red Road is the path toward redemption. As Native American brothers and sisters unite in a great circle we sing together, we pray together and we suffer together. We mentor one another and treat each other as family. We are joined together to share each other's experiences and journey. When we have a problem, we need to help each other.

Silence leads to inertia. Inertia is the lack of change and leads to sorrow and acceptance; and acceptance makes us an accomplice to our own oppression. So, we need to communicate – verbally and in writing. We need to talk about the things that no one wants to discuss. We need to write about the things that we are afraid to put in writing. We need to break the chain of complacency.

A Native American spiritual practioner's goal is to come together as a group united on the Red Road. The path won't be a lonely one, as long as we walk together.

Through the experiences I witnessed, heard of, and have been a part of, I have learned a wealth of knowledge. If I withhold this knowledge and hide under my bed, I can do my time without frustration, but I won't be at peace when I see my brothers suffer the cruel, bitter sting of oppression. What was happening to the Native American prisoners in Arizona was and is happening to Native American prisoners in every state. So, we must walk forward, walking in the rain through a field of lightning.

By standing up for ourselves we risk and lose everything they can take, but we gain much more in return. We gain footing towards the Red Road and as a group we are more connected with our ancestors. Although a boulder may be placed in the middle of the river to divert the stream, the boulder wears down over time. You must make your choice to be either the boulder or the river.

In order to create any kind of change within a system, one must generate an enormous amount of tension. There are more opponents to your actions than people willing to help. But the people who see where you are going, are the ones who will help.

Always keep writing. Read history, then start making it. Start an information network and share your struggle with the whole world. Ultimately, your biggest asset will be your actions. Follow the Red Road.

The prison is the last outpost for dignity and human survival. In this bleak place, Native American prisoners are the final guardians of the Sacred Hoop. There is no *correction* in this system, only corruption. There is no *rehabilitation* only recidivism. There is no justice, only injustice. It is up to us few, the survivors of the system and the advocates who can see where humanity is going, to stand up for the children of Mother Earth and Father Sky, for all of us.

NATIVE AMERICAN RIGHTS SURVEY

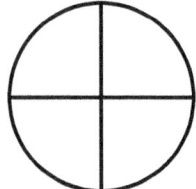

The purpose of this survey is to understand what is happening to Native American prisoners in any unit. It gives a foundation of understanding to the person interested in helping the Native American prisoner. Spiritual advisors, Native American organizations and advocates for Native American prisoners can send this survey to Native American prisoners.

Circle the answer that best describes the Native American religious rights at the prison institution at which the inmate is located.

Policy

What type of written policy does the institution have related to traditional Native American religion?

     Specific   General   None

Is the institution's religious written policy easily accessible by inmates?

     Yes   No   Unknown

Does policy guarantee Indians access to traditional religious leaders on a basis like that afforded to inmates of other religions?

     Yes   No   Unclear

Does policy allow access to sacred objects?

     Yes   No   Unclear

Does policy allow for traditional hair length for religious purposes?

    Yes   No   Unclear

Does policy allow for the wearing of head bands for religious purposes?

    Yes   No   Unclear

Specific Provisions:

Sweat Lodge

Does policy allow Indian access to a traditional Native sweat lodge?

    Yes   No   Unclear

Specify:

Frequency:

Does policy name the proper tools necessary to conduct a sweat ceremony?

    Yes   No   Unclear

Does policy provide for enough wood to conduct sweat ceremonies on a weekly (or scheduled) basis?

    Yes   No   Unclear

Does policy provide for other materials such as lava rocks necessary for the sweat ceremony?

    Yes   No   Unclear

Are proper procedures in writing in order to protect the sweat lodge and religious area from desecration?

    Yes   No   Unclear

Does policy state that the sweat lodge location be private and secure?

    Yes   No   Unclear

Religious and Sacred Items

Does policy provide proper safeguards to protect religious items?

    Yes   No   Unclear

Does policy explain specifically what a sacred object is according to Native American spiritual belief?

    Yes   No   Unclear

Does policy provide for visual inspections only, for both natural objects and blessed items?

    Yes   No   Unclear

Does policy protect the eagle feather?

    Yes   No   Unclear

Does policy protect the medicine bag?

    Yes   No   Unclear

Does policy specifically provide for access to drums?

Hand Drum	Yes	No
Water Drum	Yes	No
Pow Wow Drum	Yes	No

Does policy specifically provide for access to musical instruments?

Flute	Yes	No
Gourd	Yes	No
Other instruments	Yes	No

Does policy specifically provide for access to spiritual items?

Headbands	Yes	No
Beadwork	Yes	No
Choker / Medallion	Yes	No
Feather (Eagle)	Yes	No
Ceremonial Pipe	Yes	No

Medicine Bag	Yes	No
Bones (animal)	Yes	No
Fur	Yes	No
Seashell	Yes	No
Candle	Yes	No
Tobacco Ties	Yes	No
Medicine Bundle	Yes	No
Other Items	Yes	No

Does policy specifically provide for access to herbs?

Sage	Yes	No
Sage, various	Yes	No
Cedar	Yes	No
Cedar, various	Yes	No
Tobacco	Yes	No
Tobacco, various	Yes	No
Sweet grass	Yes	No
Kinnikinnick	Yes	No
Mint/Spearmint	Yes	No
Corn Husks	Yes	No
Corn Pollen	Yes	No
Corn Meal	Yes	No
Other Herbs	Yes	No

Comments:

Other Ceremonies

Does policy provide provisions for a pipe ceremony?

    Yes   No   Uncertain

Does policy provide provisions for a talking circle?

    Yes   No   Uncertain

Does policy provide provisions for classes or extracurricular activities for Native Americans equal to other religions?

    Yes   No   Uncertain

Does policy provide provisions for a Pow Wow ceremony?

    Yes   No   Uncertain

Does policy provide provisions for special ceremonies?

    Yes   No   Uncertain

Does policy provide for crisis counseling for Native Americans?

    Yes   No   Uncertain

Does policy provide for an overview of ceremonies?

    Yes   No   Uncertain

Other Considerations:

Does policy provide equal opportunity for sweat lodge membership at the discretion of the members?

    Yes   No   Uncertain

Does policy provide equal access to spiritual advisors and religious leaders?

    Yes   No   Uncertain

Does policy provide for equal observance of American Indian Days, September 24-25, or other tribal holidays?

    Yes   No   Uncertain

Does policy allow access to the Native American religious area equal to that of other religions?

    Yes   No   Uncertain

Does policy provide any resource or training for staff to understand Native American beliefs, such as the Sun Dance Way, ceremonial conduct and moontime traditions?

    Yes   No   Uncertain

Does policy provide provisions for Christian Indians to practice both Native American and Christian ceremonies?

    Yes   No   Uncertain

Other Comments:

FINAL WORD

The history of Native American religious practice in prison is written largely through court cases in which Native American religious rights were oppressed. History needs to be created by changing this trend and it can be accomplished through activism.

The return of religious rights for Native American prisoners will depend largely on the actions of the people. Help is needed to spread the word and it is time to *stand up for your people.*

Some of the events and names in this book have been changed to protect people from retaliation. The prison officials mentioned are not bad people within their own realm of understanding; but as I have experienced in the past, the worst kind of evil is that which is blind to its own evil acts.

Prison, ultimately, is a system based on greed. There are many individuals who profit off human misery in America and many who are selectively blind to the ways of the system. But there are those who are perfectly aware what is happening. It is up to Native Americans who have experienced injustice to share this awareness and enact a plan of change for the system. The changes that need to happen will take a lot of work and time, and the steps for change will happen slowly with great effort.

Many of my Native American brothers who were involved in the events mentioned in the book are no longer at the same facility or have been released; everyone has moved on. I too, have been released since the events took place, leaving me with my pencil and a pad of paper in order to create change for the benefit of Native American prisoners.

While incarcerated, two other Native Americans in Arizona have informed me they filed lawsuits over the desecration of the sweat lodge and their religious items. They told me privately, because they were afraid of retaliation from other brothers and the prison system. Whether they won or lost, the important thing is that they did the right thing and stood up for their religious freedom and rights; they can move forward.

This is a struggle not just for the emancipation of spiritual rights, but a struggle for the soul of humanity. Sometimes it can feel as if one step forward leads to two steps backward. The feelings of fear, desperation and disappointment may occur time after time; but keep moving forward. Any action taken is always positive, no matter the outcome. Don't let time, procrastination and inertia become an enemy of the fight. Doing nothing leads to nothing and self can be your worst enemy.

It is time to act, brothers and sisters; let's meet up on the Red Road!

We do this for our people, the Red Nation, the First People.

Aho!
To all our relations,
And the Great Spirit

Aho!
Grey Bear

ACKNOWLEDGEMENTS

Thank you to all the brothers who gave me support in many different ways throughout this experience.

Thank you to the Native American Rights Fund Library for sending me vital information to get started.

Thank you to the zine publishers who helped me publish issues of the *Native American Prisoners Journal* and to Tom Big Warrior for sending me copies of his Native American zine.

Thank you to Julie Castro at Fiesta Publishing for making my dream of publishing this book a reality.

Thank you to my family, especially to Patricia and Joshwai who are always there for me. Your support has made a difference in my life.

Thank you to my brother Walks in Faith, who first showed me the Red Road, and taught me how to sing the songs to get there.

Finally, on behalf of Arizona Native American prisoners, thank you Lenny Foster, Director of the Navajo Nation Corrections Project for setting up Sweat Lodges throughout Arizona prisons and bringing inmates together in harmony as we travel the Red Road.

ABOUT THE AUTHOR

Gabriel Sharp (Grey Bear), a Mohave Indian of the Colorado River Indian Tribe in Parker, Arizona was raised by his mother in Tempe, Arizona. From the time he learned how to read, he realized that he had an insatiable thirst for knowledge that would never be fulfilled. He had read the Encyclopedia Britannica and Webster's dictionary by the first grade. Both of his parents had master's degrees from Arizona State University, and he grew up reading books on psychology, spirituality and Native Americans. He also had a love of drawing, writing and storytelling.

At age eighteen, he joined the Army. He earned a certification as an Emergency Medical Technologist during military combat medic school at Fort Sam Houston, San Antonio, Texas; and then become certified as an x-ray technologist when he served as an Army Reservist. After bootcamp, combat medical school and radiologic technologist school, he returned to Phoenix. He trained as a nursing assistant and he worked in a nursing home for a short time.

In 2007, Gabriel was sentenced by the State of Arizona and incarcerated for ten years flat; with no chance for parole, clemency or justice. While incarcerated, he trained to become a paralegal and obtained his certificate from Blackstone Career Institute. He also obtained an Associate Degree in General Studies.

After years of religious retaliation and abuse from the prison system, he found himself at a crossroads. Gabriel wrote for the prison school's newsletter where he also taught English, so he decided to use his experience and *take on* the Arizona Department of Corrections concerning its inequitable treatment of Native American's and their religious freedom.

Released in 2017, Mr. Sharp continues his education today as he studies for a bachelor's degree in electrical engineering. He and his life partner, Patricia, have a son. He wrote the book, *Stand Up for Your People,* in hope of educating and energizing incarcerated Native Americans to fight for their rights to practice their faith to the Creator.

> *"So, from the outskirts of society, the part no one wants to admit exists, Native American prisoners find ourselves as the forgotten Americans. Racial injustice and religious intolerance thrive in America's penological system. This system profits from human misery. America has more prisoners than any other country on this planet. Many Native Americans have been incarcerated or have family members that have been incarcerated. It is time to stand up for the rights of the Native American people who are affected by this system."*
>
> *Grey Bear*

REFERENCES

1. "American Indian Spirituality Beliefs and Practices", Federal Bureau of Prisons, April 1992. Print.

2. Bahti, Tom Southwestern Indian Tribes Las Vegas: KC Publications 1968. Print.

3. Bangs, Jeremy. "The Truth About Thanksgiving Is That the Debunkers Are Wrong." History News Network, Sept. 2005, historynewsnetwork.org/article/15002. Web.

4. Beals, Janette et al. "Social Epidemiology of Trauma Among 2 American Indian Reservation Populations", American Journal of Public Health 95, no. 5 (May 1, 2005): pp. 851-859. Retrieved from: https://www.ncbi.nlm.nih.gov/pmc/articles/PMC1449268/. Web.

5. Black Elk, Recorded and Edited by Joseph Epes Brown The Sacred Pipe, Black Elks Account of the Seven Rites of the Oglala Sioux Univ. of Oklahoma Press, Norman 1989. Print.

6. Bourne, Edward Gaylord. "The Naming of America." The American Historical Review, vol. 10, no. 1, 1904, pp. 41–51. JSTOR, www.jstor.org/stable/1833813. Web.

7. Brooks, Laura. "Traveling the Spiritual Path." First Nations Issues of Consequence, http://www.dickshovel.com/nar.html. American Religious Freedom www.dickshovel.com/nar.html. 14 July 2009. Web.

8. Brown, Dee Bury My Heart at Wounded Knee New York: Henry Holt and Co. 1970. Print.

9. Bucko, Raymond A. The Lakota Ritual of the Sweat Lodge: History and Contemporary Practice. Published by the University of Nebraska Press in Cooperation with the American Indian Studies Research Institute, Indiana University, Bloomington, 1999.Cary, Harold. "First Contact with the Navajo – 1540." Navajo People Culture History, 8 May 2012, navajopeople.org/blog/first-contact-with-the-navajo-1540/). Web.

10. Congressional Record 3 Nov. 1993 S578 Religious Freedom Restoration Act of 1993. Senate Report No. 103 – 111, 1993. Print.

11. Clarke, Matt. Native American Prisoners Win Lawsuit Over Right to Wear Long Hair, Prison Legal News July, 2019. Retrieved from: https://www.prisonlegalnews.org/ news/2019/jul/2/native-american-prisoners-win-lawsuit-over-right-wear-long-hair/.

12. D'Errico, Peter. Native American Spiritual Freedom in Prison. Rev. 4 Aug 1997. www.nativeweb.org. web. 14 July 2009

13. D'Errico, Peter Prison at Night: Native Spirituality Behind Bars. 1998, www.nativeweb.org. web. 14 July 2009. Web.

14. DeVoe, J.F., and Darling-Churchill, K.E. (2008). Status and Trends in the Education of American Indians and Alaska Natives: 2008 (NCES 2008-084). National Center for Education Statistics, Institute of Education Sciences, U.S. Department of Education. Washington, DC. Retrieved from: https://nces.ed.gov/pubs2008/2008084.pdf. Web.

15. "Dogs of the Conquistadors." Weapons and Warfare, 2 Jan. 2019, weaponsandwarfare.com/2019/01/12/dogs-of-the-conquistadors/. Web.

16. Donovan, Bill "Inmate Rights Violated." Navajo Times 31 Mar. 1994. Print.

17. Doyle, Jr., Robert T. and Peter P. d'Errico Brief for Appellants, Trapp et. Al. v. Dubois, 27 Dec. 2000, www.nativeweb.org. 14 July 2009. Web.

18. Doyle, Jr., Robert T. and Peter P. d'Errico Plaintiffs Post-Trial Memorandum, Trapp et. Al. v. Dubois, 12 Jan. 2000. www.nativeweb.org. 14 July 2009. Web.

19. Dunbar, Ashley (2011) "Native Americans: A Study of Their Civil War Experience," Journal of Interdisciplinary Undergraduate Research: Vol. 3 , Article 4. Retreived from: https://knowledge.e.southern.edu/jiur/vol3/iss1/4. Web.

20. Duthu, N. Bruce American Indians and the Law. New York: Penguin – Viking, 2008. Print.

21. Dussias, Allison M. "Ghost Dance and Holy Ghost: The Echoes of Nineteenth-Century Christianization Policy in Twentieth Century Native American Free Exercise Cases." Stanford Law Review April 1997. Print.

22. Echo-Hawk, Walter, et al. "Issues in the Implementation of the American Indian Religious Freedom Act: Panel Discussion." Wicazo Sa Review, vol. 19, no. 2, 2004, pp. 153–167. JSTOR, www.jstor.org/stable/1409505

23. Echo-Hawk, Walter. Letter to Arthur Peabody Jr. 25 Jan 1996. Print.

24. Echo-Hawk, Walter. Study of Native American Prisoner Issues. National Indian Policy Center, George Washington University, Washington D.C. 1996. Print

25. Editors, History.com. "Columbus Controversy." History.com, A&E Television Networks, 27 Oct. 2009, www.history.com/topics/exploration/columbus-controversy. Web.

26. Economic Development Research Program. Arizona's Native Tribes Univ. of Arizona. 28 April 2010. Web.

27. "Environmental Justice for the Navajo: Uranium Mining in the Southwest." www.umich.edu/~snre 492/sdancy.html web. 27 May 2010. Web.

28. Fisher, Frederick. Resource Guide for the Incarcerated Native American South Chicago ABC Zine Distro 2007. Print.

29. Franklin, Catharine R. "Black Hills and Bloodshed: The U.S. Army and the Invasion of Lakota Land, 1868–1876." Montana: The Magazine of Western History, vol. 63, no. 2, 2013, pp. 26–93. JSTOR, www.jstor.org/stable/24416238. Web.

30. Ginkel, Katie, et al. "Effects." The Sioux Uprising of 1862, University of Minnesota Duluth, www.d.umn.edu/ cla/faculty/tbacig/studproj/a1041/siouxup/Effects.htm. Web.

31. Ginkel, Katie, et al. "Hangings." The Sioux Uprising of 1862, University of Minnesota Duluth, www.d.umn.edu/ cla/faculty/tbacig/studproj/a1041/siouxup/Hangings.htm. Web.

32. Goodman JM, Goodman ME. The Navajo Atlas : Environments, Resources, People, and History of the Diné Bikeyah [Internet]. Norman: University of Oklahoma Press; 1982 [cited 2019 Jul 20]. (The Civilization of the American Indian Series; vol. 1st ed). Available from: https://search-ebscohost-com.lopes.idm.oclc.org/login.aspx?direct=true&db= nlebk&AN=15354&site=ehost-live&scope=site). Web.

33. Greenfield, Lawrence A., and Steven K Smith. "U.S. Department of Justice, American Indians and Crime." Https://Www.bjs.gov/Content/Pub/Pdf/Aic.pdf, Feb. 1999. Web.

34. Guifoyle, Michael, Indians and Criminal Justice Administration: The Failure of the Criminal Justice System of the American Indian 1988. Print.

35. Harris, David A. Profiles in Injustice New York: The New Press 2003. Print.

36. Hiram Price, Commissioner of Indian Affairs, "Rules Governing the Court of Indian offenses," March 30, 1883, U.S. Department of the Interior, Office of Indian Affairs. Print.

37. Herder, Irene. Letter to Albert Hale. 16 Dec 1996. Print.

38. Horwitz, Tony A Voyage Long and Strange New York: Henry Holt and Company. 2008. Print.

39. Hutton, Paul Andrew. The Apache Wars : The Hunt for Geronimo, the Apache Kid, and the Captive Boy Who Started the Longest War in American History. Vol. First edition, Crown, 2016. EBSCOhost,search.ebscohost.com/ login.aspx? direct=true&db= edsebk&AN=1050198&site=eds-live&scope=site). Web.

40. "Interior, Justice to meet with Indians." The Washington Times 22 Mar. 1994. Print.

41. Iverson, Peter The Navajos New York: Chelsea House Publishers, 1990. Print.

42. Jaffe, Matt "Nuclear Materials 'Poison' Navajoland." ABC News 23 Oct. 2007. Web. 27 May 2010. Web.

43. The Jailhouse Lawyers Handbook: How to Bring a Federal Lawsuit to Challenge Violations of Your Rights in Prison (JLH) 4th ed. Center for Constitutional Rights and the National Lawyers Guild, 2005. Print.

44. Johnson, Marshall "Navajo Nation must move away from coal mining." The Arizona Republic 22 June 2010, B11. Print.

45. Josephy Jr., Alvin M. Ed. America in 1492 New York: Vintage Books – Random House Inc., 1991. Print.

46. King Jr., Martin Luther. I Have a Dream New York: Harper San Francisco 1992.

47. Kisto, Rose Ann. Arizona Department of Corrections Native American Religious Services Program Manual. Rev. Ed. July 1994. Print.

48. Lapahie Jr., Harrison "Narbona" www.lapahie.com 2001. 27 July 2008. Web.

49. Leland, Sue. "Information on Moontime Traditions." Earthcircle. org. 1997. The Earth Circle Association. 14 July 2008. Web.

50. Levin, David C., Curing America's Addiction to Prisons, 20 Fordham Urb. L.J. 641 (1993). Available at: https://ir.lawnet.fordham.edu/ulj/vol20/iss3/18 . Web.

51. Lewisburg Prison Project. "Legal Bulletin 2.1 Religious Rights in Prison." July 2005. Print.

52. Lowenthal, Gary T. Down and Dirty Justice. New Jersey: New Horizon Press, 2003. Print.

53. Marquis, Thomas B. Wooden Leg: A Warrior Who Fought Custer Lincoln and London University of Nebraska press 2003. Print.

54. Matthiessen, Peter. In the Spirit of Crazy Horse New York: Viking 1991. Print.

55. Milwaukee, Brenda J. Child (Red Lake Chippewa) University of Wisconsin at. "Boarding Schools." Encyclopedia of North American Indians, Houghton Mifflin, edited by Frederick E. Hoxie, Houghton Mifflin, 1st edition, 1996. Credo Reference, https://lopes.idm.oclc.org/login?url= https://search.credoreference.com/ content/entry/hmenai/boarding_schools/0?institutionId= 5865. Accessed 21 Jul. 2019. Web.

56. Multicultural Alliance for a Safe Environmental (MASE) "Uranium Mining: Environmental Racism in Navajoland." Censored News. 11 Nov. 2009. (http://bsnorrell.blogspot.com/2009/11/uranium-mining.html). 27 May 2010. Web.

57. Nell, Denise. "Rights denied to Native Americans Panel Says." University Daily Kansan 31 Mar 1994. Print.

58. "New Mexico Prisoner vindicates Native American Religious Rights with Injunctions, Fees and Damages." Prison Legal News 21.4 (April 2010): 30. Print.

59. "Outlawing American Indian Religions." Native American Netroots, 28 Feb. 2010, http://nativeamericannetroots.net/diary/380. Web.

60. "Pequot Massacres Begin." History.com, A&E Television Networks, 3 Mar. 2010, www.history.com/this-day-in-history/pequot-massacres-begin. Web.

61. "Navajo Population Profile 2010 U.S. Census." Home, Navajo Epidemiology Center, 1 Dec. 2012, www.nec.navajo-nsn.gov/Portals/0/Reports/NN2010PopulationProfile.pdf. Web.

62. Northridge, Mary A. and Peggy M. Sheperd. "Comment: Environmental Racism and Public Health." American Journal of Public Health 87.15 (May 1997): 730 – 732. Print.

63. Pellow, David Nauib and Robert J. Brulle. "Poisoning the Planet: The Struggle for Environmental Justice." Contexts 6.1 (Jan. 2007): 37. Print.

64. Polakovic, Gary. "Latinos, Poor Live Closer to Sources of Air Pollution; Health: Low-Income Neighborhoods are Exposed to Higher Concentrations of Toxic Chemicals, Study Says." Los Angeles Times 18 Oct. 2001: B1. Print.

65. Prison Activist Resource Guide, Prison Support Directory. May 2009. Print.

66. Public Law 95 – 341, 95th Congress. American Indian Religious Freedom Act, 1978. Print.

67. Schupman, Edwin. "Native Words, Native Warriors." Boarding School - Native Words Native Warriors, Smithsonian National Museum of the Native American, 2007, americanindian.si.edu/education/codetalkers/html/chapter3.html. Web.

68. Senna, Joseph J. and Larry J. Siegal Introduction to Criminal Justice, 2d ed. Minnesota, St. Paul: West Publishing Co., 1981. Print

69. "Sweat Lodge Ban Does Not Violate RLUIPA." Prison Legal News 21.4 (April 2010). Print

70. Takaki, Ronald A Different Mirror New York: Little, Brown, and Company / Back Bay Books 1993. Print.

71. The Editors of Encyclopaedia Britannica. "Auburn System." Encyclopaedia Britannica,

72. Encyclopaedia Britannica, Inc., https://www.britannica.com/topic/Auburn-system. Access

73. date September 3, 2019.

74. Tom Big Warrior "America: A Prison House of Nations and a Nation of Prisons." South Chicago ABC Zine Distro 11 June 2003. Print.

75. Tom Big Warrior. "Crime and Punishment and Still more Crime." South Chicago ABC Zine Distro 16 June 2003. Print.

76. Tom Big Warrior. Editorial. The Red Heart Warrior Allentown: Red Heart Warrior Society. Print.

77. United States Department of Justice, Federal Bureau of Prisons. Inmate Religious Beliefs and Practices 27 Mar 2002. Print.

78. Utter, Jack. American Indians: Answers to Today's Questions Michigan:

79. National Woodlands Publishing Company 1993. Print

80. Alaska Native Heritage Center Information Packet Anchorage, Alaska 2009. Print.

81. "American Indian Wars" Wikipedia. Web.

82. Arizona Commission of Indian Affairs, http://azcia.gov . Web.

83. Banks, Dennis and Richard Erdoes Ojibwa Warrior USA: University of Oklahoma Press 2004. Print.

84. Bucko, Raymond A. The Lakota Ritual of the Sweat Lodge. Lincoln and London: University of Nebraska Press. 1988. Print.

85. Crow Dog, Mary and Richard Erdoes. Lakota Woman. New York: Harper Perennial, 1991. Print.

86. Granzotto, Gianni. Christopher Columbus. New York: Doubleday. 1985. Print.

87. Kroeber, Theordora. Ishi: In Two Worlds. California: University of California Press. 1961. Print.

88. Mankiller, Wilma and Michael Wallis. Mankiller: A Chief and Her People. New York: St. Marin's Press. 1993. Print.

89. Means, Russel and Marrin J. Wolf. Where White Men Fear to Tread. New York: St. Martin's Press. 1995. Print.

90. Northcutt, Ellen Ed. And Julie Higgins. Ed Steck-Vaughn GED Social Studies. USA: Harcourt Achieve 2002. Print.

91. Philbrick, Nathaniel. Mayflower. New York: Viking 2006. Print.

92. "Pueblo." Dictionary of American History. Encyclopedia.com. 6 Jul. 2019 https://www.encyclopedia.com. Web.

93. "Report: Increases in Spending on Corrections Far Out pace Education" July 7, 2016. https://www.ed.gov/news/press-releases/ report-increases-spending-corrections-far-outpace-education. Retrieved 12/7/2019.

94. "South America." South America - New World Encyclopedia, New World Encyclopedia, 6 Mar. 2019, www.newworldencyclopedia.org/ entry/South_America#European_influx. Web.

95. Sun Bear, Wabun, and Barry Weinstock. The Path of Power. New York: Prentice Hall Press. 1987. Print.

96. Tinker, Tink, and Mark Freeland. "Thief, Slave Trader, Murderer: Christopher Columbus and Caribbean Population Decline." Wicazo Sa Review, vol. 23, no. 1, 2008, pp. 25–50., www.jstor.org/stable/30131245.

97. Tom Big Warrior. The Red Heart Warrior Newsletter. So. Chicago Zine Distro 3:2 Spring 2004. Print.

98. "Uranium Mine Near Grand Canyon Filling with Contaminated Water." Sierraclub.org, Sierra Club Grand Canyon Chapter, 20 Mar. 2017, www.sierraclub.org/arizona/blog/ 2017/03/ uranium-mine-near-grand-canyon-filling-contaminated-water. Web.

99. "Cleaning Up Abandoned Uranium Mines." EPA, Environmental Protection Agency, accessed 19 July 2019, www.epa.gov/navajo-nation-uranium-cleanup/cleaning-abandoned-uranium-mines. Web.

100. Varner, John G, and Jeannette J. Varner. Dogs of the Conquest. Norman: Univ. of Oklahoma Pr, 1983. Print.

101. Walch, Michael C. "Terminating the Indian Termination Policy." Stanford Law Review, vol. 35, no. 6, 1983, pp. 1181–1215. JSTOR, www.jstor.org/stable/1228583. Web.

102. Wiedner, Donald L. "Forced Labor in Colonial Peru." The Americas, vol. 16, no. 4, 1960, pp. 357–383. JSTOR, www.jstor.org/stable/978993. Web.

103. Williams, Joel W. Native American Rights Fund. American Jails, 2014. Retrieved from: https://narf.org/nill/documents/ 2014_MJ_Williams_Red%20Road.pdf. Web.

Court Cases and Legal Texts

1. Arizona Revised Statue 41-1493.01 (Free exercise of religion).

2. Crow v. Gullet, 541 F. Supp. 785 (D.S.D. 1982), retrieved from https://openjurist.org/706/f2d/856/crow-v-gullet, 9/21/19)

3. Hoskins v. Lenear, 395 F. 3d 372, 375 (7th Cir. 2005) 1st Amendment retaliation claim stated when prisoner lost privileges, was in segregation for two months, and finally transferred after utilizing grievance procedure.

4. Indian Inmates v. Gunter, 660 F. Supp. 394, 395 (D. Neb., 1987) aff'd Sapa Najin v. Gunter, 857 F. 2d 463 (8th Cir. 1988). The Sweat Lodge Ceremony . . . is a preparation for all other rites as well as a rite in itself. During sweat lodge ceremonies, participants experience physical and spiritual purification and are "reborn" into harmony through the use of gifts and powers that aid in prayer to the great mystery.

5. Lemay v. Dubois, 1996 U.S. District (D.Ma.) Lexis 11645, 1996 WL 463680 (prohibiting discrimination vs. Christian and Native American Religions).

6. Maria v. Broaddus, 2003 U.S. Dist. Lexis 13329 (U.S. D.C.:NY. 2003) Sincerity cannot be drawn merely from an inmate's race. Also see . . . Combs v. Correction Corp. of America, 977 F. Supp. 799, 802 (W.D. La., 1997) (Restricting the practice of the Native American Religion only to those prisoners of Native American Ancestry . . . offends the constitutional right to practice religion of one's choice.) also see U.S. v. Boyll, 774 F. Supp. 1333, 1340 (D. N.M., 1991), app. Dismd. 968 F. 2d 21 (10th Circ. 1992). There can be no more excessive entanglement of Government with religion that the Government's attempt to impose a racial restriction to membership in a religious organization. The decision as to who can and who cannot be members of the Native American Church is an internal church judgment which the First Amendment shields from governmental interference.

7. Morrison v. Garraghty, 239 F. 3d 648,660 (4th Cir. 2001) (denying possession of Native American religious items was unreasonable) also see Charles v. Verhagen, 220 F. Supp 2d 937 (U.S. D.C. Wis. 2002) the court ruled a Muslim inmate must be allowed to have prayer oil in spite of the fact it was not essential by his faith. No compelling reason to deny and not the least restrictive means.

8. Standing Deer v. Carlson, 831 F. 2d 1525, 1530 (9th cir. 1987) Statue AIRFA did not require prison officials to consult Native American religious leaders about their sect's practices.

9. The Georgetown Law Journal, Thirty-Sixth Annual Review of Criminal Procedure. 2007-36 GEO.L.J. ANN.REV.CRIM.PROC (2007) page 974 Due process rights page 953 Religious rights.

10. Wilson v. Block, United States Court of Appeals, District of Columbia Circuit May 20, 1983708 F.2d 735 (D.C.Cir. 1983), retrieved from https://casetext.com/case/wilson-v-block, 9/21/19

www.ingramcontent.com/pod-product-compliance
Lightning Source LLC
Chambersburg PA
CBHW070539010526
44118CB00012B/1176